BY MY SPIRIT

BY MY SPIRIT

Renewal in the Worldwide Anglican Church

Edited by
Bill Burnett

Hodder & Stoughton
LONDON SYDNEY AUCKLAND TORONTO

British Library Cataloguing in Publication Data

By my spirit.
1. Church of England. Renewal – Christian viewpoints
I. Burnett, Bill
262′.0342

ISBN 0 340 42537 7

CONTENTS

All biblical references are taken from the Revised Standard Version, except for those in the chapters by Canon Michael Harper and the Rev Charles Irish, which are taken from the New International Version.

THE CONTRIBUTORS

BIOGRAPHICAL NOTES ON AUTHORS
The Rt Rev Dr Bill Burnett

The Rev Canon Michael Harper

Michael is pre-eminent among Anglicans as one of the 'fathers' of the movement of Spiritual Renewal. As founder of the 'Fountain Trust' he was greatly used by God to encourage Christians to appropriate their inheritance in the Holy Spirit. He has fostered the movement of renewal in the Holy Spirit as the author of numerous books, by the organising of many conferences, which for many Christians were watershed experiences, and by a teaching ministry. His own personal Pentecost has led him to respond in obedience to the Lord's great commission, and thus to a ministry involving constant and arduous travel in continents and islands all over the world. Michael is now the executive director of the world wide Anglican agency for spiritual renewal called SOMA. (Sharing of Ministries Abroad.)

The Rev Charles M. Irish

'Chuck', as he is universally known to his friends, grew up in Ohio, USA. He served in the Marines during the Korean war, and on his return to the United States embarked on a business career. At the same time he succeeded in graduating from the Ohio Wesleyan University with a major in Philosophy. During this period he responded to a vocation to the ordained ministry. He graduated from Blexley Hall Divinity School in

1966 and was ordained in the same year. Three years later he was called to the oversight of St Luke's Episcopal Church in Bath, Ohio, where he ministered for seventeen years. St Luke's became widely known throughout the USA and beyond as a congregation being dramatically renewed by the Holy Spirit. In 1979 Chuck was appointed part-time National co-ordinator for Episcopal Renewal Ministries, and seven years later he accepted full-time responsibility for this work.

Canon Tom Walker

Tom Walker grew up in Surrey, England. He is a graduate of Keble College, Oxford, and trained for the ministry at Oakhill Theological College. Following on his ordination and two curacies, he worked for three years as travelling Secretary of the Inter-Varsity Fellowship. He was appointed vicar of St John's Harborne in Birmingham in 1970 and holds St Germaine's Edgbaston in plurality. His ministry reaches out from his parishes to the city around them. He is used in parish missions and in a Bible ministry at Conventions, with support from teams of parishioners. A fruitful link has been forged with Scandinavian Churches by means of choir tours. These have involved St John's choir, musicians, and a worship dance group, with Tom Walker as the speaker.

The Rt Rev Gresford Chitemo

Gresford Chitemo was born in Tanzania, in a village called Nyangala, in the Region of Morogoro. He received his education in Church schools and as a result responded to the Christian faith and was baptised as a youth at secondary school. Here he learned for the first time that faith meant yielding one's life to the Father and trusting in Jesus as one's Saviour and Lord. Three years later, as a student at a teachers' training college, he took this step. After another six years he responded to a vocation to serve God as a priest; and after study at St Paul's Theological College in Kenya, and later at Moore Theological College in Australia, was ordained. After six years in a parish ministry Gresford was elected as the first bishop of the new Diocese of Morogoro.

The Rev Dr Don Battley

Don Battley is a New Zealander born and raised in Auckland. After qualifying as an accountant he was prepared for ordination at St John's Theological College in Auckland and achieved his Licentiate in Theology with first class honours. After ordination and several curacies, he became, in due course, the first rector of the suburban parish of Pakuranga and served in it for twelve years. He had been acquainted with Renewal since 1966, but it was in July 1974 that, along with thirty of his parishioners, he was baptised in the Holy Spirit during a Life in the Spirit Seminar. In 1980 he initiated dialogue with New Zealand bishops over the state of Renewal in New Zealand, and with twelve other priests formed Anglican Renewal Ministries NZ in 1982, and became its chairman. Don is now Vicar of the parish of Wanganui in the Diocese of Wellington. In 1986 he received his doctorate from the San Francisco Theological Seminary with a thesis on the use of elderships, and similar corporate leadership structures in Anglican parishes in New Zealand, England and the USA. He is a member of the General Synod of the New Zealand Province.

The Rt Rev Moses Tay

Moses Tay was born of Chinese Christian parents in Johor, Malaysia in 1938. He graduated with a degree in medicine from the University of Singapore. He first practised in West Malaysia, during which time he regularly organised Scripture Union camps, and became adviser to its youth fellowships. One of these has grown into a thriving congregation. Having returned to Singapore, he specialised in internal medicine. While he served the Ministry of Health in Singapore he began a study of theology, and graduated in 1971 as a Bachelor of Divinity (Hons) from London University. He was ordained priest in 1977 and ministered as Rector of St Peter's Church Sembarang on a non-stipendiary basis. In 1981 he became Director of the Tan Tock Seng 1,300 bed hospital in Singapore. In 1982 he was consecrated Bishop of Singapore.

The Rev Graham Cray

Graham Cray first saw the light of day in Croydon near London, England, and became a committed Christian when he was eight. With school-days over, he read theology at Leeds University. On arriving at the University he joined the Christian Union which was preparing for a mission led by John Stott. Let Graham describe what then happened. 'Neither I nor many others in the Christian Union were in any spiritual condition to engage in a mission. During a series of training meetings on personal evangelism, I became deeply convicted that I had neither won anyone else to Christ, nor had seriously tried to do so. Several leaders in the Christian Union had experienced the filling of the Holy Spirit through the ministry of the South African evangelist, Ken Terhoven. In January 1966, he led a pre-term conference during which he spoke of the need to be empowered by the Spirit for witness as described in Acts 1:8. Many students responded to his message. Others of us, having missed the conference, heard the teaching on tape. In a basement flat packed with students, during a time of prayer after listening to the tape, I experienced my personal Pentecost. The reality of Jesus, His Spirit and His Word were vastly heightened for me, but the most significant evidence that God had answered my heart's cry was that I led my first friend to faith in Christ just twenty-four hours later. Shortly after, I received the gift of tongues during a time of private prayer.'

In the summer term of the same year he responded to God's

call to the ordained ministry. After a serving at St Mark's Gillingham, in Kent, he trained at St John's Nottingham. In due course he was invited by David Watson to join the staff at St Michael-le-Belfrey in York, and three years later in 1978, became its Vicar.

INTRODUCTION

THE AGE OF THE SPIRIT
The Rt Rev Dr Bill Burnett

The world-wide movement of spiritual renewal, variously described as the Charismatic Movement or Renewal in the Holy Spirit, is no mere peripheral event in the life of the Church. This is primarily so because like the incarnation, and the resurrection of Jesus, Pentecost is at the centre of the Church's experience and tradition.

The fact is that the Kingdom of God is also the Age of the Spirit. It was the King, Jesus, baptised, sealed by prophecy and the Holy Spirit, who announced and inaugurated it. So also were fulfilled Old Testament prophecies that God would pour out His Spirit upon His people to enable them to know Him and to live in obedience to Him. How otherwise could we begin to keep the impossible ethic of the sermon on the mount?

The prophecies of Jeremiah, Ezekiel and Joel about the coming Spirit announced by mere men so long ago, immediately became contemporary history when Jesus was born. They become immediately contemporary every time I lay my hands on someone, who seeking to be filled by the Holy Spirit, finds it happening. The harsh and hopeful words of John the Baptist, the last of the Old Covenant prophets, are really timeless and break upon our minds afresh as we honour today the King whose Kingdom and ministry He announced by faith. That it should be so was established when John, pointing to Jesus said: 'I have baptized you with water; but he will baptize you with the Holy Spirit' (Mark 1:8).

This prophecy began to find fulfilment in Jesus' own experience of baptism in the Jordan. To this He added His own royal command and promise to His disciples after His resurrection, namely, that they too would be possessed by the same Spirit by whom He lived and ministered as the Son of man (Acts. 1:8).

In Peter's speech on the day of Pentecost he explained that inexplicable event in Jerusalem by saying, 'This Jesus God raised up, and of that we all are witnesses. Being therefore exalted at the right hand of God, and having received from the Father the promise of the Holy Spirit, He has poured out this which you see and hear' (Acts 2:32–33). The implications are profound. If Jesus is even now baptising people in the Holy Spirit, as we see and hear Him doing, He cannot be dead. He must be risen. Since no man can baptise himself or another with the Holy Spirit, what John the Baptist said must be true. What Jesus had promised is true. What Peter preached is the truth. It happens as we pray for the anointing of the Spirit in Jesus's Name.

This is what I knew with shattering clarity when Jesus baptised me in the Spirit of His own initiative in 1972 in the chapel of my episcopal residence in Grahamstown, South Africa. The Holy Spirit given and received is also a sign of the resurrection of our King. If we pray for someone to be filled with the Holy Spirit and it happens, Jesus has done it. Faith is vindicated, and we rejoice in the reign of our King.

The movement of renewal in the Holy Spirit cannot be relegated to a tolerated 'spirituality' in the Church. The fruit and charisms of the Spirit are wholly necessary for life and ministry in Christ. This is true for another reason also. What the Lord has done in evidently manifesting His Spirit among us cannot be seen as peripheral because the number of those Christians who have consciously, however they may explain it, appropriated the Holy Spirit, has grown in less than a century to over 270 million. Only about a million of these are Anglicans, but Roman Catholics are believed to number 35 million, and very few parts of the Church remain untouched, and there are, of course the Pentecostals. Meanwhile

Western Christianity withers like the grass upon which the breath of God blows for withering (Isa. 40:6–8).

In his painful letter to the Church in Galatia, St Paul asked the Galatian Christians a simple question, to which he knew they knew the answer as recent converts to the Faith. His question would have been absurd unless they had known the answer in their own experience of initiation into Christ. The question was, 'Did you receive the Spirit by works of the law, or by hearing with faith?' (Gal. 3:2) To have asked this question, and to have expected a coherent reply, required that the Galatians, and any other Christians for that matter, could be expected to know at first-hand the when, and the how, and the results of their having received the Holy Spirit. It was not simply a teaching but a happening. To many modern Christians who know of the Holy Spirit by hearsay alone this is an inexplicable or unfair question.

The authors of this book know the answer to this question, not by hearsay, but because they too have experienced what St Paul knew his Galatian friends had received from God. We offer this book as a small contribution to the restoration of a part of our heritage as Christians, so that it may be now with us also as it was in the beginning.

Spontaneous Combustion

The movement of spiritual renewal, sometimes called the Charismatic Movement is surely unique in Christendom. It is unique in its worldwide impact and in the lay involvement it has evoked. Its genesis during the second half of this century is perhaps best described as a mighty spiritual spontaneous combustion. The fire of the Holy Spirit and the light of Christ have been manifested without synodical decisions, or the planning of departments of mission and evangelism in the Church. It is not the product of a particular notable spiritual leader or prophetic figure. In its ebullience it has flowed over the protecting walls of what we are pleased to call the mainline Churches, producing substantial and frequently lively ecclesial bodies. This book is focused, however, on some aspects of the movement of spiritual renewal within the Anglican Communion.

The largely unplanned spread of this movement of renewal within Anglicanism has been remarkable. When Britannia ruled the waves, Anglicanism was spread by military chaplaincies, missionaries and colonists in British-occupied territories. What has happened during the second half of the twentieth century, as the Holy Spirit has been poured out upon Christians, resembles much more the way in which seeds floating, as coconuts do, are carried across the oceans by winds and currents from one continent to another, where, deposited on a distant shore, they take root and spread speedily in a new environment. 'The Kingdom of God is as if a man should scatter seed upon the ground, and should sleep and rise night and day, and the seed should sprout and grow, he knows not how' (Mark 4: 26–27).

Thus it was that in an apparently random and disorderly fashion the good news of the reality of God's redeeming love, and of the pouring out of His Holy Spirit upon His sons and daughters, has been spread by priests and laity during the last three or four decades. In some places it was the clergy who were first filled with the Spirit and bore testimony to it. In others it was the laity, or perhaps the Bishop. In North America the movement of the Spirit was first manifested among students and staff in universities. Sometimes it was passed on by layfolk travelling abroad who returned with a new empowerment to share. It spread by word of mouth. It spread by people in Bible study and prayer groups speaking about the new power and joy of God which was being received. It was spread by national and international conferences, and by leaders, who, thrown up by God found themselves being invited to straddle the globe, as people young and old sought to keep abreast of what the Lord was doing.

Soma

As all this was happening a principle began to be discerned which has enormous implications. What had happened was a Divine initiative. The Christian tradition in St John's Gospel records Jesus saying, 'My Father is working still and I am working'. And, He added with His own deep emphasis on what He was about to utter, 'Truly, truly, I say to you, the Son can do nothing of his own accord, but only what he sees the Father doing; for whatever he does, that the Son does likewise' (John 5:17,19).

Thus it was that at a gathering of international leaders in Anglican renewal, immediately preceding Lambeth '78, it seemed good to those present, and to the Holy Spirit, that a movement should be initiated to provide support in the Body of Christ for what He was quite evidently doing.

This was the genesis of the movement with the significant name of Support Of Ministries Abroad (SOMA). It exists to blow glowing embers into flame, and to take the initiative in lighting new fires in obedience to the Lord's great commission to go into all the world and to continue Jesus's work of making disciples (Matt. 28:18–20). It is not possible for people in many third world countries to invite and finance visits from leaders in renewal to encourage and to teach. So SOMA seeks to travel where the Lord calls to provide support. With a minimum of financial support, but substantial faith, Canon Michael Harper accepted responsibility for undertaking what have proved to be truly apostolic labours. Ten years after SOMA was born there are four or five SOMA missioners based in the USA, Canada, Australia and, of course, Britain.

SOMA does not mean to try to do the job alone. It encourages parishes and dioceses to catch the vision, and some parishes have. Teams of lay people led by their priests respond to invitations to share with diminished or newly established congregations what the Lord has done among them. In Singapore, for example, a rector has led teams of his parishioners who, taking their annual leave to do so, and paying their own way, have borne much fruit for the Kingdom by ministries in West Malaysia and the Philippines and elsewhere in South East Asia.

When many more congregations renewed in the Spirit catch this vision, the revival of the Church becomes possible with all the attendant opportunities for profound social consequences. The response to the movement of the Holy Spirit is evidence of a spiritual hunger of millions of people in the West as elsewhere.

All Over the World

God knows what is happening in Fiji or in Tanzania or Calgary or London as His Spirit moves among people there, but we do not. It has seemed good and necessary therefore to make it possible for a wider public to catch a glimpse of how things appear, and of what is happening as the Lord brings things old and new out of His treasury for blessing all over the world.

In this book we have brought together essays by authors in Asia, Africa, New Zealand, the United Kingdom and North America. They write for the most part as those engaged in parish and diocesan renewal. Others take a glance at renewal in the context of ecumenism and of social righteousness.

I would have wished to have been able to include more than two chapters by Christians of other than a Western cast of mind. Christians from another culture are frequently able to bring to light, without any didactic intention, issues and spiritual truths of which we may be unaware. It may even be that their method of presentation of the faith may have something to say to us, in spite of their having written in a second language. Western people generally present what they have to say in somewhat linear and abstract patterns. A progression of ideas which may seal out the imagination is expected. An African mind is rather more diffuse in its presentation and progresses in a more circuitous fashion. It is less abstract and more situation and people orientated, and in this as well as in its tendency to repetition, it resembles Old Testament authors.

Bishop Chitemo's contribution is as packed with events as the gospels are, and like them has an underlying theology which is frequently implicit rather than explicit. I have regretfully found it necessary to 'straighten out' the African form of expression to accommodate the somewhat one-dimensional Western mind.

Signs of the Kingdom

The chapter on a renewed community as a sign of the Kingdom of God is not a concession to the secular mind of the twentieth-century Church. On the contrary it is a way in which we consider how to relate the Christian faith and experience to everyday life as we seek to serve the world in the Name of Christ. The Church is to be a sign of the Kingdom. It does not exist for itself. When, like Jesus, we entrust our lives to the Father in the obedience of faith, we find that He begins to do through us, what He began to do in Israel and beyond. This can best be described as nothing less than the healing and the gathering of the nations to present them as a redeemed people to the Father. In participating in this we give expression to His righteousness, because it is His ministry. We have no ministry of our own. How else could Jesus have said, 'Truly, I say to you, he who believes in me will also do the works that I do' (John 14·12). St Paul elaborated, saying of his ministry: 'For this I toil, striving with all the energy which he mightily inspires within me' (Col. 1:29).

The essay devoted to this theme takes us at once to the root of the Christian's social responsibility within his family, village or town, his place of employment or his country. We are directed to the Lord's Prayer:

> Thy Kingdom come,
> Thy will be done,
> On earth as it is in Heaven.

We are pointed at once to the righteousness of the King, who, in due course will present a redeemed world to the Father. The prayer Jesus taught us to pray is undoubtedly eschatological but it also anticipates realisation of the King's righteousness here and now.

When we address ourselves to the question of what is the righteousness of the King we discover it cannot find direct ideological expression because it is neither simply an idea nor is it a social structure. The Church itself is not the Kingdom nor is any society it may devise. It is perhaps significant that the new Jerusalem of the Book of Revelation is depicted as coming down out of heaven from God. It is not our Kingdom but God's gift to us. This may sound somewhat nebulous but the righteousness and power of the King is nevertheless available to us and substantial. God made Jesus 'our wisdom, our righteousness and sanctification and redemption,' said St Paul (1 Cor. 1:30 and 2 Cor. 5:21). Since He alone is our righteousness it is only by receiving His own Spirit, by whom are conveyed both His love and power, that we may express His righteousness. We cannot conjure up these gifts of God. They are conveyed by Him. They are known in relationship with Him. They are, in fact, God with us. Consequently we can have no righteousness of our own which is anything other than a delusion.

We must expect to see some evidence of God's Kingdom and His righteousness. This is all the more necessary since St Paul, in Colossians, declares boldly that all power and authority has been created 'through him and for him' (Col. 1:16). Unfortunately, between that creation event and the incarnation all authority having become deranged, as it was exercised in a multitude of structures by sinful men, authority itself has had to be brought afresh under the authority of the King who 'disarmed the principalities and powers and made a public example of them, triumphing over them in him.' (Col. 2:15). This is, of course, the only way in which deranged authorities can be renewed and become a reflection of the Kingdom. They must be brought into submission to the Lord. This has become possible because 'the ruler of this world is judged' (John 16:11) and we are redeemed by the King.

It is surely a kind of midnight madness for Christians who, one must presume, believe in the essential and unique redeeming power of the Lord Jesus Christ, to suppose otherwise. It is also naïve, on the other hand, to suppose that children of God in the process of appropriating their heavenly inheritance will not frequently succumb to the wiles and lusts of what St Paul called the ruler of this present evil age. Being, alas, by nature idolatrous ourselves, and living among many who do not acknowledge the King, we are unlikely to be able to bring deranged authorities into full submission to the Lord. That must await the Lord's final coming in glory. The best we can do, therefore, even in societies in which Christians are numerous, is to use a godly pragmatism as we seek earnestly to live by the ethic of the Kingdom, of which the sermon on the mount is a sample, and which is, to frail man, an impossible ethic.

We who exercise authority in the Church ought to know this. Our idolatries, both personal and corporate have torn the seamless robe of the Fellowship of Christ into a multitude of unrelated rival 'authorities'. How is it then that we expect governments to do much better!

One of the thieves crucified with Jesus seemed to have penetrated the mystery of our redemption when he shouted, 'Jesus remember me when you come as king'. We need not doubt that his prayer was heard. We need not doubt, moreover, that Jesus is aware of our constant need of Him. The breathtaking truth is that He who is our righteousness not only offered the perfect obedience of an unblemished sacrifice that we might be counted righteous and justified by faith in Him; He not only conveys to us the status of sons and daughters, but also what we need quite as much, namely, the substance of sonship. He gives us His Spirit to convey to us His righteousness. Jesus came also 'in order that the just requirement of the law might be fulfilled in us, who walk not according to the flesh but according to the Spirit' (Rom. 8:4). He gave us the Holy Spirit at Pentecost. So we begin to receive the substance of our inheritance when, making space for His Spirit within us, we die to sin a little more each day and arise refreshed in the vigour of His righteousness.

Jesus began and completed His ministry under the anointing of the Holy Spirit. The anointed One was led ineluctably to complete His baptism in Jordan on the cross on Calvary. As He approached Jerusalem for the last time He cried out, 'I came to cast fire upon the earth; and would that it were already kindled! I have a baptism to be baptized with; and how I am constrained until it is accomplished!' (Luke 12:49,50).

The same Spirit is given to us. He leads us to the same place. This is why Paul exhorts the Philippians to 'Have this mind among yourselves, which is yours in Christ Jesus, who, though he was in the form of God, did not count equality with God a thing to be grasped, but emptied himself taking the form of a slave' (Phil. 2:5–7). His mind becomes our righteousness, as we empty ourselves and take the form of a slave. This is the way we live the life of the baptised. This is what St Paul meant when he wrote: 'I have been crucified with Christ; it is no longer I who live, but Christ who lives in me' (Gal. 2:20). This is what baptism in the Spirit is all about. I have discovered that one of the mysteries of God is that He spells slave 'son'!

Social and Political Righteousness

Jesus' righteousness, which is both the obedience of faith in, and the supreme expression of, the undeserved love of God, demands much more of us than what we understand as justice. It invites us to fulfil the New Commandment. We are expected to lay down our lives for the brethren, and to share our good things with them. Perhaps because we have done so little of that the 'outsiders' become determined to take from us what we do not share. This is called a revolution.

It has for some time been the fashion to say that the agape love of God can only be filtered into the structures of society as justice. That is dubious to say the least. The Western mind has spread the notion widely that God's righteousness can be spelled 'justice' and that justice means egalitarianism. This concept of justice is an unattainable ideology. It is perhaps a figment of the imagination. History gives us no example of its realisation. But once justice (egalitarianism) is identified as the righteousness of God it becomes a 'sanctified' ideological power for driving men to hate and even to kill one another. It creates a climate for jihad. God's righteousness is not egalitarian. How odd of God to choose the Jews. How unfair of God to allow widely different gifts of intelligence. A definition of justice might well be, 'An eye for an eye and a tooth for a tooth'; but even then it is possible to complain that the quality of the eye I have removed from my enemy is nothing like as far-sighted as the one he removed from me! It is not helpful then to find that most recent translations of the New Testament translate the word righteousness (Greek: Dikiosune) as justice.

It would seem that the meaning of righteousness in the New Testament holds in tension God's act of salvation, and the standard of ethics which is the outcome of it, like the turning of the other cheek and the going of the second mile and forgiving one's enemies.[1]

How then do we apply the righteousness of the King to social and political decision making? Some would conjure up once more the theory of the Natural Law. When, however, we affirm a New Covenant within which the righteousness of Jesus is the norm for Christian living, it is inconsistent to revert to a theory of a Natural Law in public life. Then the agape righteousness of the King is relegated to some sort of irrelevant counsel of perfection.

What is more, one can make of the so-called Natural Law what one likes. It defies definition. Doubtless we should know the law of God as a part of His creation, but the moral blindness of fallen man prevents it. The use of the Natural Law as a yardstick frequently opens the way for the insinuating of various religious absolutes into contingent moral judgments. Public decision-making consistent with the righteousness of our King, requires a godly pragmatism in the context of the righteousness of the King. This is so because there are no political absolutes. By a godly pragmatism I do not mean a moral complacency, but a serious attempt to insinuate as much of the righteousness of Christ into the law-making processes of sinful men as possible. Because we affirm the unique sufficiency of God's righteousness in Jesus Christ we avoid abandoning His 'agape righteousness', and the ethic of the Kingdom. Thus we do not revert to a simple application of law, whether the Natural Law, so-called human rights, or an egalitarian ideology. It is the righteousness of Jesus, who has fulfilled the law, which must govern our law-making processes as it is filtered as much as may be into the many and various structures of society.

Unity and Disunity

In the letter to the Ephesians, Christians are exhorted to be 'eager to maintain the unity of the Spirit in the bond of peace'(Eph. 4:3). Unity is one of the marks of the Church of God, and a sign of the Kingdom. The Holy Spirit has been described as the means by which the Lord cements the Church in fellowship.

Reading recently an abridged version of John Wesley's journal, I came across an account of how he accompanied George Whitfield and heard him preach on the theme of the Holy Spirit. He went on to say thereafter that they had both been censured for their preaching by those who preached as though there is no Holy Spirit. In another place a gentleman who had previously received him with marks of affection and approval now cold-shouldered him, remarking that a mutual friend, who had been at Wesley's college at Oxford, had told him that John had always been a little crackbrained. And even George Whitfield took Wesley to task on account of the outward signs such as falling under the power of the Spirit, shaking and trembling, and weeping and groaning under a deep conviction of sin, which frequently accompanied his preaching. But that very day while Whitfield himself preached such signs were manifested![2] When there are evident signs of the power of the Spirit among us, after the first sense of surprise and even shock, we do not find it difficult to recognise them and be thankful for what the Lord is doing. Yet when these things only happen when others preach and pray, we think they are very dangerous indeed!

Thus it was when, without my asking, I experienced a flooding of my life by the Holy Spirit in 1972, and shared the joy and wonder of it with the bishop with whom I enjoyed the deepest of relationships, he was silent for a space, and then said, 'You have made me a second-class Christian.' I could not understand it then, but I do more easily now, because since then I have become aware of twinges of jealousy and of a sense of having been left out when I see others exercising spiritual gifts which have not come my way. This, of course, is sin. I ought to have glorified God for the gifts He gives to men. But even as we invite the Holy Spirit to bring more of our lives under the lordship of Christ, and so grow in grace more than hitherto, we remain redeemed sinners with nothing to contribute to our salvation but our sin.

Incidents like these illustrate the fact that when revival begins in the Church, all sorts of presuppositions are shaken. Things we once took for granted are no longer the same, and hurts are received where no hurt is intended, and yet we see and hear, and share in the glory and blessings of God in a way we could not hitherto have imagined. Simply to become aware that the manifestations of the Holy Spirit in the ministry given us are the intervention of God Himself, is very humbling but glorious.

In the diocese of Singapore where the Bishops have been in the forefront of renewal in the Spirit, and almost all the clergy of the Diocese have responded to the Lord's renewing grace, unity in the Holy Spirit is clearly evident. With other Churches in Singapore which are experiencing the same blessing, there exist also beautiful relationships in the Holy Spirit across ecclesial structures.

In New Zealand, which is the context for Don Battley's

chapter, the struggle for the movement of renewal in the Holy Spirit to flourish has, as in many other parts of the Anglican Communion, been tough and sometimes even painful. This has by no means always been the fault of Mother Church. It is nevertheless true that in some parts of the Church its implicit or even overt resistance to what the Lord has been doing, as He has poured out His Spirit on many of our people, has contributed to the growth of new Pentecostal bodies. Some of these have, alas, shown a distressing tendency to foster further divisions.

One of the perplexing phenomena I have observed in many parts of the Anglican Communion has been the apparent inability of the hierarchies to perceive why certain parishes are growing in membership; are strongly supported by men as well as women and young people; are active in sharing the faith in obedience to the great commission; are examples of strong lay participation in ministering the gifts of the Spirit; and are more socially aware than most other parishes. At the same time they out-give other congregations in a dramatic fashion. Why is it that we do not perceive the hand of the Lord in this, more particularly when there is, in many parts of Anglicanism, a continuing shrinkage in membership? Are we afraid that the Spirit who is the wind who blows where He chooses, might take us where we do not wish to go?

Why are we unable to grasp that what is happening as the Spirit breathes His life into His people, is simply what He did in the beginning, when the risen Lord poured out His Spirit on the day of Pentecost? While we fail to recognise this, it ought not to surprise us if many tell themselves, that since it is no longer now as it was in the beginning, they might as well bale out, and find an ark of salvation more like the one launched in the fire of Pentecost in the beginning. But this is all so unnecessary because potentially the Anglican structure could provide an almost perfect vehicle for the Spirit of God to use to His glory. This would require that we give Anglicanism back to God to use as He may choose. He wants His Church back.

No Mystical Experience

Some Christians are distrustful of any claim to experience a relationship with God. It is thought, at best, to be the product of a dubious subjectivity. A relationship with the living God is, however, never simply subjective. It is never anything less than a relationship with God initiated by Himself, and corroborated by Holy Scripture.

We do not therefore describe in these pages some mystical experiences suited to people of a particular temperament or spiritual intensity, but of the proper inheritance of every Christian, from every candidate for confirmation to every Archbishop. Like St John we write about that which we have seen and heard: 'so that you may have fellowship with us; and our fellowship is with the Father and with His Son Jesus Christ' (1 John 1:3).

Notes

1. See article by N. H. Snaith in *A Theological Wordbook of the Bible*. Edited by Alan Richardson, p. 205 (SCM Press 1950).
2. Charles Wesley and George Whitfield *The Nature of Revival*. Edited by Clare George Weatley Jr pp. 140–1 (Bethany House Publishers, Minneapolis, 1987).

THE GREAT COMMISSION AND PENTECOST

THEORY AND PRACTICE

The Rev Canon Michael Harper

Some opponents of Christianity would like us to accept that in the West Christianity is a thing of the past. They refer to 'post-Christian Europe', for example. But this is to be defeatist and inaccurate. Europe has never truly been a Christian society except in name. We need to be people of hope who are always looking forward to and expecting the Kingdom to come in power, whether it is in Africa, Asia, Europe or North America. In that respect we are all in the same boat. And great though progress has been in the Third World, we must not exaggerate it. After all, Africa is still fifty per cent pagan.

We are now within sight of the end of the century, and even more fascinating, of the second millennium. It is, therefore, interesting to look back to see how Christians viewed the end of the last century. Pope Leo XIII, whose pontificate bridged the two centuries, is best known for his encyclical, *Apostolicae Curae* which pronounced Anglican orders invalid in 1896. But it was he, standing at the door of the twentieth century, who prophesied that it would be a century for the fresh honouring of the Holy Spirit.

The end of the last century was also a time of fervent prayer for revival. Pentecostals claim the last day of the nineteenth century (31st December 1900) as the start of their Movement. That evening Charles Parham laid hands on Mrs Agnes Ozman during a prayer meeting at his Bible School in Topeka, Kansas. As the clock struck 12.00, ushering in the twentieth century, Agnes spoke in tongues. The Pentecostal Movement, which has now encircled the globe and has over 150 million adherents, had begun.

At the time no one would have connected the Pope in Rome with Charles Parham in the United States, but in 1975 St Peter's Basilica in Rome was filled with 10,000 fervent Roman Catholics singing in tongues in the presence of Pope Leo's successor, Paul VI. There was a connection after all.

The year 2000 will not only be the end of our turbulent century and the beginning of the twenty-first, it will signal the end of the second Christian millennium and the start of the third. There are already signs that the significance of this is engaging the attention of Church leaders. Dr Billy Graham has indicated that his organisation has plans for the use of satellite technology for a new surge of evangelism throughout the world as the century runs its final course. Roman Catholics have already designated the final decade of this century, 'a decade of world evangelisation'. Charismatics now have a similar focus, and both the European ACTS 86 conference, which drew nearly 8,000 Christians together from all over Europe in July 1986, and the New Orleans American Conference in 1987 chose evangelisation as their major theme. There is a possibility of world gatherings in 1990, and of the final decade of the century having a special focus.

Already there is a growing conviction that God wants to mobilise the Churches, renew them in the Holy Spirit, equip them with His power, for a huge spiritual harvest by the year 2000. Tom Forrest, a Roman Catholic priest, has a vision for one billion converts by the end of this century. How can these dreams come to pass?

A Coming Harvest

I believe we should see the whole of the twentieth century as preparation for this coming time of harvest. Huge strides have taken place in technology – the car, nuclear power, jet propulsion, space explorations, radio and television, computers, heart transplants, telecommunications, etc. But during the same period there have been two world wars with massive loss of life. Auschwitz and Hiroshima have gone down in history as human holocausts which have caused immense suffering. The world map has been largely re-written, with changes in frontiers, some countries shrinking in size and some disappearing for ever, others being enlarged at the expense of their neighbours. Many new nations have arisen, notably Israel and the nations of post-colonial Africa. New scars have marked the landscapes of the world, the Berlin Wall and Chernobyl being particularly significant.

But all this is only the back-cloth to the real drama which has been going on: the emergence of new Churches, evangelisation on a scale hitherto unimagined, the use of radio and television, the Ecumenical Movement, the Second Vatican Council, the re-awakening of the Church's social conscience, and the re-equipping of the Churches with spiritual power and gifts, so that our century may well go down in history as the Pentecostal one.

We have touched on the major influences in the twentieth century. But what lies ahead for us? In what ways will the twenty-first century be different? If we are to follow the Lord Jesus Christ faithfully in the coming years, we need to be clear that it will not be by technology, socio political action (however laudatory), painstaking dialogue or sheer human effort that the Kingdom of God will come. It will be *by God's Spirit.*

The twentieth-century focus on the Holy Spirit has restored, where He has been honoured and received, important dimensions for evangelism and mission. This should not surprise us when we examine the record of the New Testament. All four Gospels record, with differing details, the 'great commission', and all, with the possible exception of Matthew, maximise the role of the Holy Spirit in the fulfilment of that commission. Mark mentions the signs which 'will accompany those who believe'. These signs are described elsewhere in the New Testament as 'gifts of the Holy Spirit'. They are designated in Mark's Gospel, primarily as functions of evangelism, for we are told that the disciples preached everywhere and, 'the Lord worked with them and confirmed his word by the signs that accompanied it' (Mark 16:20).

Luke, who records in detail the event of Pentecost, mentions the words of Jesus that they are to preach in His name, but to wait in the city 'until you have been clothed with power from on high' (Luke 24:49). Again we see Pentecost as a 'mission event'. In Acts, Luke further underlines this by quoting the words of Jesus, 'you will receive power,' and 'you will be my witnesses' (Acts 1:8). In John, the upper room commissioning for mission is accompanied with the words 'Receive the Holy Spirit' (John 20:22). So far as the record of the 'great commission' in Matthew is concerned, although there is no mention of the Holy Spirit as such, the promise recorded in 28:20, 'surely I will be with you always, to the very end of the age,' exactly describes the ministry of the Holy Spirit, because it is the Holy Spirit who provides the omnipresence of the Lord.

It is difficult to see how anyone can escape the conclusion that evangelism and mission can only succeed when the Holy Spirit is honoured, and his constant empowering sought faithfully by all the Churches. A proof of this is to be found in the remarkable success of Pentecostal Churches throughout the last eighty years on every continent of the world. These Churches have taken these words to heart, appropriated the promises and obeyed the commands. God has honoured their faith and commitment with much success.

The Charismatic Renewal has brought the same truths to bear within the historic Churches, and similar results have followed. Those who prophesied the end of this movement in the early eighties have manifestly been proved wrong. *Only when the whole Church has embraced and experienced these truths will such a movement become redundant, and we are still a long way from seeing that*. But the next decade and the new century will see a much greater extension of this experience amongst a far wider segment of the worldwide Church.

The Right Methods

It is important that we do not divorce the divine provision of power from the human response to it, and our need to discover (also from the Holy Spirit) the best possible methods, and the proper use of technology to achieve the goals which the New Testament has outlined for us. The early Christians certainly knew and experienced the power of Pentecost, but they were no fools. They also developed a strategy for spreading the Gospel and extending the Church which was effective. Roland Allen's famous book, *Missionary Methods, St Paul's or Ours?*[1] develops this thoroughly, and it was this book (and his equally helpful *Spontaneous Expansion of the Church*[2]) which inspired Vincent Donovan to do his pioneer work in Tanzania. He has written about this in his own book *Christianity Rediscovered*. 'The main and general insights and questions of this remarkable man,' he writes of Roland Allen, 'are as valid today as they were when they first stunned and disturbed the Church of his day'.[3] Vincent Donovan quite rightly eschewed a slavish following of Roland Allen. It would be equally wrong to follow Paul's first-century methods. No, we are to find the Holy Spirit's *present* plans for San Francisco and Santiago, Accra and Amsterdam, Bangkok and Birmingham. He is the missionary Spirit, and He will reveal the way for us as He did for Paul, provided we are prepared to do the unusual and break new ground. This may be dangerous and unpopular, and we may well suffer the consequences.

World evangelisation is a costly affair. If we are right in supposing that the Holy Spirit is putting His spotlight on a new tide of evangelistic effort, then we need to count the cost before we get too carried away. David Barrett has come up with alarming statistics about global Christianity, which should shock us into action. According to his figures only five per cent of global Christian giving goes to world mission. Ninety-five per cent is spent on the home Church scene. Americans are rightly praised for their generosity, but their giving for overseas work is even less – only three per cent. We need to evaluate this also in the light of other figures Dr Barrett gives. Christians now number thirty-two per cent of the world's population, but receive sixty-two per cent of the world's income and spend ninety-two per cent on themselves.[4] *This needs to be radically reversed.* There needs to be a redistribution of financial resources (as well as manpower), if God's call to us is to be obeyed. That means spending less money on home evangelism and giving more time and finance for the world's spiritual needs.

We are often being exhorted to give to appeals for refugees and famine relief. And so we should. *But we must also give sacrificially for the spiritual famine of the world.* And there is a connection between the two. When revival and spiritual blessing come to the Third World we can expect a change in behaviour – less corruption, greed, and war, leading to increased food production and a fairer distribution of it. But we should expect similar results in Western countries as the Gospel spreads. We have our own forms of corruption and consumer greed. The Gospel should release more finance as Christians learn to live more simply.

In the West we need a radical new assessment of our spiritual, social and financial priorities if we are going to take global evangelisation seriously. Simply talking about it is not enough. Paul wrote, 'the kingdom of God is not a matter of talk, but of power' (1 Cor. 4:20). We get nowhere if we merely talk about it. An American pastor of a growing and successful church once told an audience that the Lord had said to him, 'You are not growing, you are just getting fat'. Church growth in the West needs always to be put in the context of the world scene, and what may be praiseworthy when seen in a local situation, can be sinful indulgence in the global context. A well-known bishop once said this grace at a large civic function during World War I: 'Lord, forgive us for feasting while others starve.'

At the moment, as we have seen, the Third World is getting only the crumbs which fall from the rich man's table. Yet there are Western countries which are being saturated with the Gospel. In North America billions of dollars are poured every year into Christian radio and television. Is it right to continue to lavish money on comparative luxuries, when the most elementary needs are not being met in the Third World? Professor Robert Lyon of Asbury Theological Seminary in the United States, quotes a *Wall Street Journal* report on 'an evangelical revival sweeping the nation, but with little effect'. He comments, 'I sense a basic flaw . . . evangelicalism, for all its evidence of success and strength . . . has presented little more than a baptised version of western culture . . . it did not represent a threat to the really entrenched sources of power that belong to this world.'[5]

My wife and I belong to a small church in rural England. For many years we have had no buildings other than the ancient church itself for our meetings. Recently the church school building, close to the church itself, has gone on the market, and after much prayer it was decided to find the money to buy it. For the first time for many years the church was involved in a major capital expense. Few people would have questioned the correctness of going ahead with buying this property; it was a golden opportunity. But the church council made a decision that some of the money raised should go overseas, so that we, who have so much, could contribute to the needs of those poorer than ourselves. It was decided that out of every three pounds given, one pound would go to causes in the Third World. We are a small church, but if every church adopted this attitude it could revolutionise the world-wide Church and provide the finances to see rapid strides in world evangelisation.

When Jesus was commissioning His disciples for their world mission, He indicated that their ministry was to be similar to his:

1. As He had done works of power and mercy, so they would (John 14:12).
2. As He had been hated and misunderstood, so would they (John 15:18).
3. As the Father had sent Him, so He was sending them (John 20:21).

4. As He had proclaimed the Kingdom, so this was to be the cornerstone of their teaching and practice. They were to *do* the Kingdom as well as preach it (Matt. 24:14).
5. As He had received the anointing power of the Holy Spirit, so would they (Luke 3:22, Acts 1:8).

The Acts of the Apostles was a continuation of Jesus's ministry. He had taught that it was expedient for Him to go, so that the Holy Spirit's power could be released upon the whole Church.

Jesus linked the Kingdom of God with the signs and wonders that He performed. This is particularly explicit in Matthew's Gospel. In 9:35 there is a link made between the 'preaching of the good news of the kingdom' with 'healing every kind of disease and sickness'. He then spoke of a bountiful harvest and the need for 'workers' to go into it. The same statement is made in Matthew 4:23.

In Matthew 10:1 Jesus called the twelve and sent them out with authority to 'drive out evil spirits and heal every disease and sickness'. He went on to tell them they must 'preach this message: "The kingdom of heaven is near"' (10:7). Then follow further specific commands which include 'raising the dead'.

There is an even more explicit link of the Kingdom of God with the deliverance ministry in Matthew 12:28, 'if I drive out demons by the Spirit of God, then the kingdom of God has come upon you'. The expulsion of demons *is* the coming of the Kingdom of God.

All this is linked into what is known as the 'great commission' in Matthew 24:14 when the Lord says, 'this gospel of the kingdom will be preached in the whole world as a testimony to all nations' . . . Having demonstrated the signs and wonders of the Kingdom in his life and ministry, He now declares that the same message, and presumably the same signs, will be a testimony to the whole world. In John 14:12 Jesus had said, 'anyone who has faith in me will do what I have been doing. He will do even greater things than these, because I am going to the Father'. Jesus expects his disciples to continue his ministry of signs and wonders. But it is more than authentication of the Gospel message. It is part of that message, and to leave it out is to emasculate it.

A New Focus

'Signs and wonders' has become a new focus for the Charismatic Renewal. It made the headlines when it was included as a subject at Fuller Theological Seminary in Pasadena, California. According to Peter Wagner the course (called MC510) came out of the reaction of Third World students to the various courses on Church growth by Dr Donald McGavran. The students while expressing appreciation of the Fuller courses pointed out that something else was happening in the Third World that Western theologians and missiologists were ignoring – enormous Church growth of a first-century type. So McGavran visited Asia and Africa. He found the reports true. In many cases indigenous evangelists prayed for the sick; they were healed and an astonishing number of conversions resulted.

The course was taken by a man called John Wimber, who had been, in his own words, 'fished out of the pagan pool' some years before while a member of a music group called, interestingly, 'The Righteous Brothers'. Although this course is no longer part of the Fuller training programme for world missions, it introduced a whole new shaft of light on the subject when John Wimber insisted on practising 'signs and wonders', not just talking about them. From 1982 onwards John Wimber and others have introduced a new dimension, which has been called by Peter Wagner 'the Third Wave'. (He regards the Pentecostal Movement and the Charismatic Renewal as the other two.)

For our purposes the importance of this is twofold. First, 'signs and wonders' in the New Testament are to be seen mainly in the context of evangelism. They are signs of the Kingdom, evidences of the presence and power of God and the Messianic claims of Jesus Christ. The inevitable result of such a focus is a new surge of interest in and commitment to world evangelisation. 'Signs and wonders' are not for the converted but for the lost. The other important factor is a new desire for Christian unity. When the Church turns in on itself, focusing on its own life, then controversy reigns. Christians will argue eternally on subjects like biblical prophecy, water baptism, church government etc. But when the Holy Spirit turns the spotlight on evangelisation, He also lays the need for unity on the people of God. Evangelism without unity and holiness can be another form of hypocrisy.

Bias to the Rich?

When Bishop David Sheppard's book *Bias to the Poor* was published in 1983 I took issue with the author regarding the book title.[6] Although substantially agreeing with the main thrust of the book, I quoted Leviticus 19:15: 'Do not pervert justice; do not show partiality [bias] to the poor or favouritism to the great, but judge your neighbour fairly.' When Bishop David replied I was flattered to learn that the last time he had that text quoted at him was from the Chief Rabbi![7] I still find the phrase 'bias to the poor' difficult. In his letter David Sheppard pointed out that the Hebrew word 'tsedeq' has a persistent tendency 'to topple over in favour of those in dire need'. But we can miss the whole point by concentrating too much on the meaning of words, however important they may be. *The plain fact of the matter is that our western society has a distinct bias to the rich*, and this can be a hindrance to world evangelisation. We are now in a position in which much of the wealth of the world is in the hands of Christians, and most of the unreached peoples of the world are poor, and that is a factor which should not be ignored.

It is true that the sharp edge of the Gospel can be blunted and becomes ineffective when it is politicised. Many critics of 'Liberation Theology' would make this point. Vincent Donovan writes that 'the gospel cannot be identified with any social, political, or economic system . . . it is dangerous to preach the gospel as part of any system. The gospel is lost through such an identification'.[8] Whether it is Liberation Theology or the Prosperity Gospel, truth is perverted when it is confused with culture. Neither the capitalist dream of free enterprise, nor the Marxist utopia of the classless society is to be confused with the Kingdom of God.

Having said this, we need to recognise that it is impossible to divorce any programme for world evangelisation from its worldly setting. In Central and South America it is virtually impossible to be genuine in one's Christian calling and not be committed to changes in society, when the poor are shamelessly exploited. The Church's encouragement of anti-Semitism down the centuries has put major barriers in the way of its mission to the Jews. The West's uncritical support for the Stae of Israel, and Christians' ignoring the legitimate rights of Palestinians for self-determination constitutes another barrier to evangelism amongst Arabs in the Middle East. Evangelism in the inner cities of the West should not ignore the plight of the powerless, but needs to identify with them if they are to be reached with the Gospel. A Gospel which is identified almost entirely with the rich and powerful will make no headway in the Third World.

Truly democratic institutions are comparatively rare amongst the nations of the world. This is true not only of Communist countries in Eastern Europe, Africa and Asia, but also of many of the new nations of Africa, which are one-party states in which the media are controlled by the government, and where there is little opportunity for individuals to criticise or change the government. In these circumstances the role of the Churches becomes even more important. With the degree of immunity Christian leaders often have, they can be the only voices heard speaking out against injustice and corruption. That voice must be heard. If it is muted then the Gospel will inevitably be compromised.

Pentecost was for the world, not the Church. Whenever the Church selfishly uses the power of the Holy Spirit for itself, that power is withdrawn. The Spirit challenges us to leave our comfortable pews, and move out to where people are, and to stop preaching to the converted. The Spirit of prophecy is not given to us to make facile political statements, but to get to the heart of the matter and to prescribe the only lasting cure offered to man, the death of Jesus on the Cross. There is no other way, and the chief benefit of Pentecost is to point us all in that direction.

My Pilgrimage

Renewal is the stuff of dreams and visions. That is what Joel prophesied, and that is what came to pass on the day of Pentecost. When my wife and I experienced our own renewal in the Spirit in 1962 we were quite lonely and isolated. There was not yet much substance to show for what we believed and what we had experienced. So for some years it was a matter of 'dreams and visions'. Now we have seen these come to pass, not only in our own lives, but in thousands of others.

As Christians my wife and I were raised in the hothouse atmosphere of University Christian Unions. Some of what we experienced seems quaint to us today, but we are grateful for what was instilled into us from the beginning, 'Christianity is for sharing'. We had a vision for the world from the moment we cut our spiritual teeth. So it did not take us long to put the same into practice from the moment we were renewed in the Holy Spirit. We were not to hoard what the Lord had given to us, but share it with everyone who would listen.

The pattern of Pentecost is so simple and natural. Friends and neighbours first, then one's race compatriots, then expatriots, and finally to the ends of the earth. In other words, in ever-widening circles of influence. So we began with the people we knew in the church where we were members, and our friends in various parts of the country. Then to our Anglican Church family, our ecclesiastical 'race'. Then wider to other Churches, and finally to the whole world. We were guided in 1964 to set up the Fountain Trust, which became the spearhead of renewal in Britain in the sixties and seventies. It became also a model for other organisations which sprang up all over the world. It kept us busy sharing what we had learnt with leaders in many countries.

In 1975 we felt we needed to concentrate on our own Church family, and seeds were sown which eventually produced SOMA (Sharing of Ministries Abroad). Originally SOMA set out to share the blessings of the Renewal with the whole Anglican Communion; we are still doing that, and we now have ministries operating on all six continents. But in 1983 we combined with other Churches for a Conference in Kenya, and more and more SOMA operates in co-operation with Christians from many different Churches.

Some years ago I had a vision which has inspired me ever since, and been the controlling principle of all that I have tried to do. I saw a large company of people spread out over an extensive area. They were all working on a project, apparently oblivious to each other. They were working as individuals, and as a result there was a lot of confusion and bad relationships. Everyone was falling over everyone else, and there was much duplication of effort and, therefore, waste. It seemed impossible to call such large numbers of people to order.

Then I realised that the greatest problems in life can be overcome *provided they can be broken down into small enough units*. No one person could bring unity to such a mass of people, but every person could extend the hand of friendship to the few nearest to them, and if everyone did it eventually the whole body of people would be reached. So we begin with those nearest to us, and extend the hand of friendship, and encourage others to do the same. The Lord has not given to any one person responsibility for the unity of the Christian Church or the evangelisation of the whole world – only one small part of it. I have tried to be faithful in extending the love and grace of the Lord as wide as possible, *and to keep going wider*. In spite of all the disappointments, we must never give up.

Steps Forward

Where is the Charismatic Renewal going in the Anglican Communion? One way of plotting its course is by reference to an Anglican Evangelical Conference (NEAC) held every ten years in Britain since 1967. At the first conference held at Keele University the programme contained no reference to the Renewal, but it was freely acknowledged that it came top of the hidden agenda. Everyone was talking about it, and small informal prayer meetings took place. At the second, held at Nottingham University in 1977, it emerged from the shadows and was given some public prominence. I was invited to contribute (albeit on another and 'safer' subject!), and a song of the Renewal was the hit tune of the conference. In 1988 the whole subject has moved nearer to the centre of the stage. Some of us will be doing a major seminar (on the subject itself this time!), and there is a seminar on the controversial subject of signs and wonders.

One can trace a similar progression at the Lambeth Conference. In 1968 few had even heard of the Renewal. In 1978 there was an unofficial prayer meeting for renewal every day, which some of the Lambeth bishops regarded as a life-line, but in 1988 it is near the centre of the programme, with an introductory book called *Open to the Spirit* with contributions by Bishop Moses Tay and myself. The plain answer to the question, where is it going, is 'where the Holy Spirit wants to take it' – to the heart of the Church. It may be taking a long time, but the Renewal is on course and pointing in the right direction.

One final warning. The Holy Spirit, as this chapter makes plain, wants us on the frontiers of the world. He is the 'cutting edge' of the Church's mission to the world. He withdraws once we turn that 'knife' inwards on ourselves, or use it to fight our fellow Christians. When that happens, the glory departs.

Notes

1. R. Allen, *Missionary Methods, St Paul's or Ours?* (World Dominion Press, 1960 [1st Edn 1912]).
2. R. Allen, *Spontaneous Expansion of the Church* (World Dominion Press, 1960 [1st Edn 1927]).
3. V. Donovan, *Christianity Rediscovered* (SCM Press, 1982 [first published 1978]).
4. D. Barrett
5. From article in *Transformation*, October 1986.
6. D. Sheppard, *Bias to the Poor* (Hodder & Stoughton, 1983).
7. Letter from David Sheppard, 1st September, 1983.
8. See V. Donovan, *Christianity Rediscovered* p. 164.

THE RENEWAL OF CONGREGATIONS

INSIGHTS FROM ST LUKES, OHIO, USA

The Rev Charles M. Irish

'They called it "The Baptism in the Holy Spirit,"' an Episcopal missionary wrote. 'This experience has profoundly changed both my prayer life and my understanding of Jesus' life, death and resurrection. It has changed my whole outlook on the Bible, religious life, my Church and my calling. In fact, it is safe to say that only my name has survived intact.'

Discouraged and Disillusioned

The joy expressed by this missionary is similar to that which I felt after God rescued me from a desperate situation. I was contemplating leaving the priesthood, for it seemed as though God had abandoned me. Only a few years previously, I had driven home to tell my wife, Jan, that God had spoken to me and that she should get ready because we were off to seminary. Her immediate response was an assuring, 'It's about time'. Now, only four years after I had been ordained, I was telling her how disillusioned I was with being a priest, and how I thought I should quit. This time her response was, 'I think you should, I don't like it either'. My problem had affected both of us.

I had expectations about God. I expected to experience the same supernatural ministry that blessed the early apostolic Church. But during my four years as a priest I hadn't seen anything happen. I had never experienced the joy of seeing a person being converted to Jesus Christ, nor the transformed life of which the Bible spoke. I never saw God heal anyone of anything. I became disillusioned and discouraged because the promises of God never came true – as far as I could tell.

I found it more difficult to go through the motions each Sunday. My preaching was no longer motivated by the same conviction with which I began my ministry. I soon wondered if it was all a sham. The people seemed to be 'religious' and 'sincere', but their Christianity didn't cause them to be any different from other people in our community. The worst thing was that my life wasn't any better than theirs. I was teaching things I didn't believe any more.

For some reason, other clergy did not seem to be concerned in the same way. They appeared to believe the best about their church members even when the worst things were happening. A 'God's in His heaven and all is right with the world' attitude. It seemed to me they were oblivious to the symptoms of apathy, atrophy, and apostasy. But then, I was looking in a mirror. I was face to face with the truth of my own impotent ministry. It was a bitter pill to swallow – I was becoming a failure, and I didn't know why. I had never been a failure before.

Knowing that my ministry was not fruitful, I behaved just like many other clergy who were discouraged and disillusioned with their ministries. I asked to be transferred to another church. I didn't tell the Archdeacon that the reason I wanted to be transferred was because I was a failure and didn't want to be found out. On the surface, I had done a reasonable job in my first church. There was an increase of money and members, the measuring stick for ministry success. It was easy to get a new call. However, my arrival at St Luke's Episcopal Church in Bath, Ohio, was not the blessed relief for which I had hoped.

St Luke's had its share of modern problems. Dissatisfied with its previous vicar, they had persuaded the authorities to get rid of him. This caused a split in the congregation which contributed to mistrust among the people. There was an abundant share of alcohol and drug problems which afflicted any affluent society in the late sixties. Family life was disintegrating and children were more rebellious in this generation. God did not seem to have any answers for these situations and the Christian Church of this era became more and more irrelevant. Its ministry, content and style seemed to exacerbate the problems I was facing.

It seems strange to say that the Church of the sixties and seventies was irrelevant, especially when it was involved in almost every important social issue of the day. But instead of bringing God's redeeming and renewing life into a world desperately needing it, it brought the life of the world into the Church. I needed, as did the members of my congregation, God's answers for my life. We, clergy, were now taking people to the world because we, ourselves, had no answers.

My life and ministry reflected this Christian malaise. I had done all that the Church had taught me to do and it had produced no fruit. I even did the trendy things, thinking that in that way I might find God; again I came up empty. I was hitting rock bottom and there was no one to whom I could turn. I was aware that if I had gone to the Church authorities in my need, they would have had no more of a solution to my problems than I had myself. They would have simply sent me to a psychologist or psychiatrist. I had a spiritual problem which only God could cure, and He didn't seem to be around. The only solution available to me was to leave the priesthood, lest I be a hypocrite by professing what I no longer believed. I had, ironically enough, begun to consider the possibility of psychotherapy as a future career for myself.

God to the Rescue

On a Thursday evening in December 1970, God moved to rescue me from my decision to leave the priesthood and become a psychotherapist. Soon my experience paralleled that of the missionary I spoke of at the beginning. God's hand, I learned, was still upon me. He had not abandoned me. Through a strange series of God's 'coincidences', and through my wife's insistence, I found myself talking with a young Methodist couple in my office. I was investigating some strange religious things they were promoting in our local public school.

My daughter, Tara, had attended a Campus Life meeting and had come home shaken by the experience. Crying, she reported that all the people were 'speaking in tongues'. They told her that she could do it too, but she wasn't able. This really upset Jan and she became determined that I should be the one to straighten the people out and get it stopped. Because of her insistence, I called up the couple and told them that I wanted to talk with them about what they were doing. That was *my* mission; the young couple had another.

'Could we tell you what God is doing around the world today?' the woman asked. She caught me off guard. This was something I had not expected. I thought we would be talking about speaking in tongues, but she wanted to talk about God. I hadn't talked much about God before. I talked a lot about the Church but not about God – especially not about Jesus. She began to describe how God was pouring out his Holy Spirit in churches throughout the world. She talked about people being converted to Jesus and how their lives were being changed radically. She talked about how people were being healed of all kinds of infirmities. Her words matched the hunger in my heart. This was a divine appointment, but I didn't know it. I didn't know how to respond to what I was hearing. I had never heard a priest or bishop talking about the same kinds of things.

After telling me many wonderful things, the woman asked if they could pray for me. Again, I was caught off guard, for no one had ever asked if they could pray for me. Little did I know how this prayer would change my life and my ministry. She began to pray to God in a personal manner, as though Jesus were there listening to every word. During her prayer she reached out and touched my shoulder. I was never the same again. God filled me to overflowing with the presence of his Holy Spirit. Soon afterwards, I was speaking in another language – one that I had never learned. I didn't fully understand what this was all about, but I was about to find out.

I went home that night with the praises of Jesus on my lips. The joy of the Lord was erupting from deep within me. When I awoke in the middle of the night, I found that I was still praising Him. Sometimes it would be in tongues and other times in English. It seemed so natural and right to praise God in this manner I wondered why I had never done it before. In the morning, I had the desire to speak in tongues again, and did so as I drove the car on an errand. When I returned to the church, I found myself shouting praises to God.

The Good News Spreads

On that same morning, I had the occasion to meet with a young woman about her emotional difficulties. She had been in psychiatric care, yet her life was a shambles. The only hope, as she saw it, was to end her life. I found myself asking her a question that I had never asked anyone before. In fact, I did not even know that I could ask such a question. It was: 'Do you know Jesus?' This was not the normal question to ask of a person who was contemplating suicide, especially one who was a life-long Episcopalian. Little did I know then that she did not have any relationship with God. She had been 'sacramentalised', as some have said, but not 'evangelised'. In a short time she was on her knees confessing Christ and receiving Him into her heart. Then, dramatically, she was filled with the Holy Spirit and began to speak in tongues. She did not need to return to the psychiatrist.

It took a few days for this to sink into my mind and heart. Though I was walking in unfamiliar territory, it was a joy because I was walking into my hopes and dreams for ministry. I was now seeing people converted to Jesus Christ. I was seeing lives changed by the power of God's Holy Spirit. At first I became a bit angry at the Church because I had needed an outsider to lead me in this apostolic way. Unfortunately, that anger remained with me for almost three years. Then I discovered that I should be thankful to God for changing me and my ministry and not judge the vehicle through whom the change came. I was thankful that Pentecost had arrived in my life and that I had experienced what the apostles had experienced. I no longer wanted to leave the priesthood. I now had a reason to continue and I knew that God was fully in it.

Soon, many people from the congregation were converted to Jesus Christ and were filled with the Holy Spirit as they experienced their own Pentecost. Their lives were being changed and evidence of this fact could be seen in their behaviour. People began to be healed in various ways, including a blind woman who received her sight. Those were exciting times.

Jan had her life changed also. As she described it; 'At the time I asked the Lord for this gift of His, I was well on my way to being a "drop-out" Christian, Episcopalian and clergy wife. My encounter with Jesus Christ, through the baptism in the Holy Spirit, started an unravelling of my somewhat satisfactory, but empty, life into a blessed and abundantly-alive life.' Then, one by one, each of our four children was converted to Jesus. They, too, were filled with the Holy Spirit and spoke in tongues. It was a blessing to see how significantly their lives were changed in this process.

Others experienced similar changes in their lives. One person, who later became a priest, described his situation in this way: 'Then came December, 1971. Out of nowhere, for no reason and completely unexpectedly I was in the midst of what can only be described as a nervous breakdown. Abject hell on earth! Total horror! The extremes of mental anguish! Why? Only God knows. All that I knew was that it seemed more than I could bear. A couple of times in the days and weeks that followed, I contemplated suicide to the point of digging out one of my guns and staring at it for hours, unable to complete the intended action, without knowing why.'

The Lord placed His hand upon this man and turned his life around. 'After meeting with Chuck Irish and some of the others a few times, it readily became apparent that there was only one course of action for me to take. On Friday, January

14, 1972, at the altar rail of St Luke's, I gave my life to Jesus Christ, accepting Him as my total Saviour, begging His forgiveness for my sins, rebuking the Devil, and receiving the baptism in the Holy Spirit. Overnight my life changed. Now my life is blessed more than I previously could have imagined.'

Ministry Lessons

To enable me to help people become converted to Christ and be filled with the Holy Spirit, God taught me some important lessons. It began with my concern with the fact that most people did not change after they were baptised. Children who were baptised and confirmed, often left the Church after they came of age. There was no evidence that they were 'regenerate' as the Prayer Book described. I concluded that there was a missing link and that without it, baptism was not efficacious. C. B. Moss' book, *The Christian Faith*, helped confirm my observations. He said that, 'The practice of infant baptism was not intended for the children of parents who had no intention of bringing them up as Christians.' Then he offered this word about the effect of baptism. 'Every person who is baptised receives the new birth; but the new birth does not always develop into Spiritual life.'[1] I now wanted to know why a person's baptism did not develop into spiritual life.

God gave me two insights which helped me to answer that question. First, He showed me that spiritual life is developed when people are converted to Jesus Christ (consciously turning their souls to Him). Thus, unless the conversion takes place, and there is an interaction between God and man, there is no provision given for growth in new life.

Knowing that it was my task to find out where people stood with God, I often asked the question, 'Tell me, what is your relationship with Jesus?' This tactic proved to be both exciting and profitable, because it produced results. On one hand, hesitation or embarrassment were tell-tale signs of spiritual problems. On the other, those who had a satisfactory relationship with God were usually ready to talk about it without embarrassment.

It was soon evident to me that without a relationship with God, there was no healing for a person's life situation. When a person came into my office for any kind of counsel or confession, the first question I asked concerned his or her relationship with God. If their relationship with God was not good, and most weren't, I told them something like this: 'Look, God is the only one who can bring healing into your situation. I have nothing to give except what He is able to give. If you are willing to turn to God through Jesus, then I am able to help you. Otherwise, I have nothing to give and will have to refer you to a secular counsellor.' I only remember one person who refused to be reconciled to God when they understood the conditions.

The second insight which God gave me was an awareness that few baptised and confirmed Episcopalians had a good relationship with God. It seemed that clergy had expected too much from the sacraments, and too many assumptions were made about people's spiritual health. Few people had been led to the Lord so that they could drink from the well of salvation. This was true about the people at St Luke's Church. As a result, most often their baptisms had not developed into spiritual life. They were spiritually empty and thirsty for living water. I found this out through their own testimony. Almost every time I asked about their relationship with Jesus, the truth was revealed, and the harvest field was ready.

I learned that when a person has the experience of being born again, he or she will know it, and it will not be some sort of vague guessing game or blind confession. It will be evident by the action of God in their lives and the changes that come as a result. Clergy need to do a little more enquiry into people's lives so that they can discover what their experiences with God are. The people I asked were always thankful that I loved them enough to do so.

Along with these insights God gave me a desire that filled my heart, to see the entire congregation come into a relationship with Him and to have their lives changed accordingly. To help in this, I kept score on a sheet of paper. I wrote down every member's name and put two columns beside them. One column was for those who declared that their relationship with God was good, that they had in fact been converted to Him through Jesus. The other was for those who claimed that they had been baptised in the Holy Spirit for ministry power. Always, it was their judgement, not mine. As they told me, I marked it down, hoping for the day that all of the lines would be filled. It still seems strange to me that the Church keeps records concerning a person's baptism and confirmation, but no records about their conversion to Jesus and their growth in new life.

I put a special stress on getting the vestry members converted, since they were the leaders of the congregation. I believed that until they were reconciled to God and filled with the Holy Spirit they would stand in the way of the renewing changes that were taking place. I thought that my first victory had come when half of the vestry people had been converted and empowered. It didn't stop vestry arguments, but now there was little likelihood that the congregation's renewal would be sidetracked.

These three gifts caused me to double my efforts to see each person come into a good relationship with Christ. I evangelised them in the counselling office, in the hallways, at the altar, from the pulpit, through books, through tapes, and by bringing teachers to help us. The fruit of these efforts was substantial.

The Spirit is Poured Out

The baptism in the Holy Spirit and the teaching about the gifts of the Spirit opened the door to conversion and renewal in our church. Occasionally, I asked someone to come and do what we called a 'Holy Spirit Teaching Mission'. I advertised the events broadly throughout the entire community and with the other priests of our diocese. I sent out leaflets that asked such questions as, 'Would you like to know about the power of the Holy Spirit?' and, 'Would you like to know about the gifts of the Spirit?' Especially effective was this statement: 'Come and learn about speaking in tongues.' People wanted to know about these things and would fill our church for every meeting. The results were outstanding.

The Rev George Stockhowe was one of our earliest teachers. When he came, he would teach for ninety minutes in a rambling style. No one moved as he told about how the Holy Spirit is still being poured out upon all who are called into God's Kingdom. He taught that Jesus is the only way to the Father and that each must be converted to Him. He described what the baptism in the Holy Spirit and gifts of the Spirit are all about. I thought it amazing that people sat so quietly when they used to be impatient with twenty-minute sermons. At the end of this period, George asked people if they would like to be filled with the Holy Spirit, and if they did to come forward to the altar.

Scores of people came forward for George's altar calls. When they were there, he would do some additional teaching, usually moving from one scripture verse to another. He led them to the passages that described how the Father's promise of the Holy Spirit is given so that people can be effective witnesses of Jesus Christ. But in order to have this equipping they first had to be converted to Jesus. They were admonished to turn to God through Jesus, confess their sin, renounce the effect of the world, the flesh and the devil upon their lives, and to receive Jesus into their hearts. Then they were led to make this a public confession. Once they had done this, they were then encouraged to ask Jesus to baptise them in the Holy Spirit. Immediately, many began to speak in tongues.

Once, a man came to one of the meetings, went up for the altar call, and said, 'I don't mind being filled with the Spirit, but those tongues, I don't want them.' My experience with tongues was so positive that I could not believe anyone would refuse them if they knew what they were all about. I had pored over the Scripture to learn more about them. To my amazement, I discovered that there are two kinds of tongues.

One is private and accompanies the baptism in the Holy Spirit. About its value, Paul said that anyone who speaks in tongues is not speaking to people, but rather is speaking mysteries to God (1 Cor. 14:2). Then, he told why. 'He who speaks in a tongue edifies himself' (1 Cor. 14:4). I already knew it, Paul only confirmed it. I could understand easily, now, why Paul 'bragged' that he spoke in tongues more than anyone (1 Cor. 14:18). It was for personal edification. Paul, however, was quick to point out that personal edification, as good as it may be, must also turn into edification for the Church body (1 Cor. 14:5–12). The public gift of tongues, therefore, needs an interpretation to make it useful. The private tongue is of no value to the Church and one should refrain from making a public spectacle of it.

Because speaking in tongues is good for people, I encouraged everyone to speak in the language of the Spirit that was given as a result of their baptism in the Holy Spirit. I told them that if Peter, James and John needed their Pentecost and enjoyed the edification which came from speaking in tongues, then we needed it even more. I told people that God would not overpower them and embarrass them, for the tongue was always under their control. They could start and stop any time they wished. The disciples spoke in tongues 'as the Spirit enabled them' (Acts 2:4). How wrong the translators are who think of tongues as 'ecstatic utterances', or something resulting from a trance.

From what I can determine now, tongues are either earthly or heavenly languages. It is fun to see how God confounds those who believe none of this is for real. The first person in our congregation to pray for baptism in the Holy Spirit during a public meeting sang a beautiful song in tongues. 'She is praising God and glorifying the Trinity in Italian,' another person exclaimed, who understood Italian because she was raised in an Italian family. But the woman who sang did not understand a word of Italian. Another time a man began to speak in tongues at the altar rail. The person next to him, a Catholic priest and a scholar, said, 'It's beautiful, it's beautiful, he's praising God in Hebrew.' On another occasion, as I was praying with a woman, I began to speak in tongues. The woman looked up at me in shock. 'You are speaking Japanese,' she said. This woman had lived in Japan for a number of years.

Before the Lord sent that young Methodist couple into my life, I was like the Sadducees who were in error because they did 'not know the Scriptures or the power of God,' (Mark 12:24). When I was baptised in the Holy Spirit everything changed. Since that time I have prayed with hundreds of priests whose ministries have come alive after they were empowered by the Holy Spirit.

Once, three Byzantine Catholic priests came to our altar to ask Jesus to baptise them in the Holy Spirit. They were disillusioned with the ministry, and were on a leave of absence so that they could decide whether or not to remain in the priesthood. As they were filled with the Spirit the Lord made their decisions for them. Two remained in the priesthood, of whom one became the president of a seminary; the third became a full-time lay church worker. Each one would tell you that his Pentecost experience changed everything for him.

The fact is that God wants each one of us to receive his baptismal inheritance. What this is Paul clearly described in the letter to Titus: 'He saved us through the washing of rebirth and renewal by the Holy Spirit, whom He poured out on us generously through Jesus Christ our Saviour' (Titus 3:5–6). The same twofold inheritance of the Christian is neatly described in Galatians 4:6. 'Because you are sons, God sent the Spirit of His Son into our hearts, the Spirit who calls out, "*Abba*, Father."'

Because this is the twofold gift of God to those who are initiated into the Body of Christ, and all must surely come to know when they have received what St Paul calls 'the promised Holy Spirit, who is a deposit guaranteeing our inheritance' (Eph. 1:13–14). I always tell those whom I have led to Jesus that there is more for them to receive. In response to this I find almost everyone has wanted to be assured of their personal Pentecost. The results have been impressive. It has been just as the Word of God described it. God did not give them a stone or a scorpion, but more of the Holy Spirit (Luke 11:9–13). He gave them their own Pentecost provision.

Moving from Personal to Congregational Renewal

Because significant changes had taken place at St Luke's our life came under the scrutiny of many who came to see what was happening. Our small congregation, it seemed, was being viewed by the world. It is understandable when one considers the changes. Our budget had risen from $17,500 to $240,000, and finally to over $500,000. Our congregation was fortieth in member size in the diocese, but fourth in total giving. Our worship was exciting; people were being healed, and there was plenty of lay ministry. In addition we began to spawn new congregations.

Over the sixteen years in which I was involved with the renewal of St Luke's, I began to develop teaching programmes, so that others might learn from our experience. Soon, I also was involved with Episcopal Renewal ministries and spent a lot of time travelling around the United States, sharing insights about renewal. The following are some of those insights in the form of 'steps in congregational renewal'.

Personal renewal is the first step in congregational renewal. There is no way to get around it. Unless people are evangelised and converted to Jesus Christ, there is no possible way to have the fruit of the Spirit evidenced in their lives. We cannot assume that baptism will do the job without evangelism. The renewal efforts of many clergy have failed because they neglected to lead people to Jesus Christ. Since most clergy do not know how to evangelise their own congregations, they may have to study under those clergy who are manifesting this gift.

The second step in congregational renewal is getting the people baptised in the Holy Spirit, so that they are more effective in their various ministries. There is a simple way of discovering if people have, in fact, been empowered with the Holy Spirit to minister. Ask them if they have received all the spiritual power they need to perform the supernatural ministry God is requiring of them. If the answer is 'Yes', then rejoice. If it is 'No', then encourage them to ask Jesus to baptise them in the Holy Spirit.

The third step in congregational renewal is to develop a vision for the local congregation. Through prayer and listening to God the pastor of a congregation should be able to determine, in part, the expectation God has for the life of that local group. This leadership function cannot be consigned to one's spouse, prophecy group, or to a visiting teacher. For some time, I did not realise the importance of this part of leadership. As a result, people often did not know what to expect. I soon learned that God is very specific and will not impose a smörgåsbord of directions for the local congregation so that people can pick and choose what they want.

At a vestry retreat, my former associate, the Rev Ronald Jackson, challenged me to tell the vestry what the vision for the congregation was. At first I was upset, because he had corrected me, but finally I saw the wisdom of the Lord in what he said. I wrote down the four specific things I knew God expected of the congregation, and presented them to the vestry. They were visibly relieved to hear the specifics. Then I was able to demonstrate how lay ministry would be released among us as the vestry members became responsible to add to and enflesh the vision.

Establishing a vision is easier when we look at the Church through the eyes of God. A Pentecostal minister gave me a tremendous insight into doing this. He said that, with the Lord, we should consider the answers to four basic questions:

1. What kind of Christian does God expect our Church to send into the world?
2. What kind of Church must we be to produce that kind of Christian?
3. What kind of leaders must we be to produce that kind of Church?
4. What kind of pastor must I be to produce that sort of leader?

This was a completely new concept to me, since I had always looked at the Church from my own perspective. I used to encourage members to do the same by sending them questionnaires that asked what they expected of the Church. It was popular during this time, to use the industry model of long-range planning. The best that this did was to get the people serving their own wills instead of the Lord's.

As things changed, and we began to seek God's will instead of our own, strangely enough my own authority as priest and rector was increasingly recognised. We were soon pulling together in one direction, and so it became easier to lead the people. And since, moreover, the vestry increased in prayer and in listening to God, they participated in the vision by adding to it and by ratifying it as their own.

The fourth step in congregational renewal is to provide basic teaching for the congregation. This means starting from the beginning, and teaching the basic biblical themes of the Church. As people are converted and filled with the Holy Spirit their hearts and minds need to be cleansed and refreshed with God's Word. New converts are usually eager to learn as much as they can. Even though they may have heard the same things before, they will hear as though for the first time.

The fifth step in congregational renewal is to disciple its leaders. Ours were the vestry. I began by reminding them that our work was not to be obedient to the will of the people, but rather to the will of God. This meant that we had to learn to listen to God, and tell one another what we thought God was saying. We operated under a unanimity rule that meant there would be no decision unless we agreed on God's mind for us.

Soon, it was necessary for our vestry to meet once a week. As part of the discipleship of the vestry, it was important that our meetings focus on God and what He was doing. This helped us keep our vision straight. The following is a general outline of our meetings:

1. Praising God in word and song
2. Bible teaching

3. Responses to the teaching and its meaning to our congregation
4. Testimonies about what God is doing among us
5. Thanksgivings to God
6. Praying and anointing for the needs of the vestry members
7. Praying and anointing, as a 'James Five' eldership, for those people in the congregation who came to us with needs
8. Business
9. Minutes and treasurer's report

The next task was that of educating the members of the congregation to be more discerning in their selection of vestry members. By holding before them the criteria for good leadership, they had values to help them in their selections. Soon they were electing those who were converted to Christ, baptised in the Holy Spirit, showed signs of Christian maturity, known as leaders, and dedicated to the vision for the congregation. They tithed and were willing to give the time that it would take to serve on the vestry. This made for a very effective leadership.

The sixth step in congregational renewal is to get lay ministry started. At the beginning, I included lay people in almost all of the ministry that I did. If I led someone to the Lord, I would include the lay people in the prayers. If I was counselling someone, I would have a lay person counselling with me. If I did a teaching mission elsewhere, I took them with me and included them in the ministry. Soon, they were becoming more confident and were willing to risk more, for they saw that God was willing to manifest Himself through them. Then, I was able to launch them into ministries of their own. At one time over one half of the people were serving in ministries.

I saw that my primary task was to prepare and release people to do what they were called to do. I was an enabler. That meant that I had to take an inventory of those ministries that I thought belonged to the lay people. This was necessary so that I didn't encroach on their territory. My list of lay ministry included: visiting the sick and shut-in, praying for and anointing the sick, blessing houses, calling on new people, calling on members, meeting people in their crisis situations, interceding in prayer, pastoring people, counselling people, and administrating the affairs of the church.

The big test for lay ministry came when my counselling load became greater than I could handle effectively. The vestry agreed with me that it was time to release the responsibility for church counselling into lay hands. At first, we thought about hiring a professional, but then we realised that God equips His people to do this work. When I was ordained, I was not equipped to counsel people. I set out to give people a much better preparation than I had. Twenty-four lay people were trained to be spiritual counsellors. When they were ready, all of my counselling load was shifted into their hands, and I did almost none. The lay people were effective with both routine and crisis counselling. In fact, they were so successful that other clergy sent their difficult cases to us.

The seventh step in congregational renewal is to develop meaningful *koinonia* or fellowship. We found that very difficult since we didn't have an adequate vision for small groups. Ron Jackson again came to the rescue. He had a vision for fellowship groups which were to become the pastoral arm of our congregation. Ron took six lay couples and gave them the experience of what he called a house church (not to be confused with those in England.) During this experience, he taught them how to become pastoral leaders.

When the leaders were ready, we encouraged interested members to attend one of the groups. Overall it was a success. As the leaders practised what they had learned, their effectiveness increased. The house churches became places where people brought friends and neighbours to witness the loving care shared there. Some groups grew so large that it was necessary to prepare new leaders. The groups not only provided the front-line pastoral care for our congregation, but they also served to unite people around the common vision of the church.

There is no adequate way to stress the importance of getting church people converted to Jesus Christ and to be filled with the Holy Spirit. If God had failed to intervene in my life to show me His way, I would be immersed in humanism. My life would have been included as one more number with the millions who have already given up on God and the Church during the past few decades.

I speak to those who are on that edge, who are disillusioned with ministry and who are ready to throw in the towel. Don't do it, but turn to someone who is experiencing the fullness of God in their ministry and ask them for help. God has an abundance to pour out in your life. I know that I am still learning what that abundance is all about, but this time my lessons are exciting and full of God.

The principles I have described are but one way to talk about congregational renewal. There are others and other leaders to teach them. What is important, however, is that all be done with the gentleness of strong love. To do this, leaders must cease to see others as adversaries and, instead, see them as objects of love, those to be served. The most loving thing that can be done for anyone is to lead them to Jesus.

Notes

1. C. B. Moss, *The Christian Faith: An Introduction to Dogmatic Theology* (Morehouse-Gorham, 1954).

PARISH RENEWAL

INSIGHTS FROM BIRMINGHAM, ENGLAND

The Rev Canon Tom Walker

The apostle John gave the precedent for personal testimony when he wrote 'that which we have seen and heard we proclaim also to you' (1 John 1:3). The sharing of personal experience among Christians can be an enriching and stimulating exercise, so I do not shrink from explaining something of my own pilgrimage which lies behind the patterns of shared, every-member ministry, which have evolved in St John's Harborne and St Germain's Edgbaston in Birmingham. My disappointment with the Church of England in its heavily structured and institutionalised form has led to an attempt to loosen our rigid forms in working for Church growth and prayerful outreach into a largely unbelieving community. The testimony which follows is not only about a personal encounter with God, in Christ and through His Spirit, but also about the corporate experience of His working in our Church.

The First Look

'Come and see what it's like', my eight-year-old friend pleaded. He had just joined the choir at St Martin's, Dorking, and was longing to have another new boy to keep him company. Actually, this was not my first look at the church, because my parents had taken me to Evensong for at least two years. But although I enjoyed the music, which was of an exceptionally high standard, I did not find 'church' an enthralling experience. I had the impression that I was 'to be seen and not heard' for most of the time. My impression of the church was the same as that of a teenager quoted in the report *Teenage Religion*[1]: 'You find nearly all old people going to church because I think they want to get on the good side of God before they die.' This was an unfair criticism for me to make, since many younger people were caught up in the war effort, and most young men were fighting in the armed services for the cause of freedom.

As I grew up in the choir, the discipline of three, sometimes four, intensive practices per week, plus several demanding choral services on Sunday (not to mention weddings on many Saturdays), led to a deep commitment to the life of the church. The progression from choirboy to choirman and later organist, intensified this loyalty to church life, but sadly it was an outward and superficial commitment and at that stage did not lead to a personal faith in Christ. Indeed there was a further complication during my teenage years, because I became attracted to a pretty young Sunday School teacher who used to sit with her Sunday School children in the front row of the church. I was in the choir stalls, straight in line with what seemed to me to be a beatific vision! My motives for church attendance were now totally corrupt. I was paid to play the organ and sing in the choir. I was drawn by the presence of this charming member of the opposite sex. I enjoyed the performance of cathedral-style music. It could be said that I only attended church because of money, music and women! I eventually settled the last of these wrong motives by marrying Molly Anne in that same parish church on 6 July, 1957.

But even during those early years of church-going there were moments when my own standing with God was challenged. The curate who prepared me for confirmation queried my bad behaviour in the confirmation classes. He went so far as to suggest to my parents that I was not a suitable candidate to be presented to the bishop. In fact, my outward bravado was only a cover-up for the fact that inwardly I was desperately serious in my search for God. Several times I was made to think earnestly about a call to ordination, but I could not understand those who testified to a personal call to the ministry. An ordinand once wrote of his experience in the *Sign* parish magazine insert, 'God spoke to me directly.' I thought, 'How ridiculous! How can God speak to anyone personally like that? But,' I mused, 'if he ever does speak to me in a personal way about a call to ministry, I shall have to take it very seriously indeed.' Looking back on these early days of church-going, I am full of gratitude for an upbringing that wedged me firmly in a Christian environment. However, I often wonder what would have happened if I had gone forward to train for the ministry from the position of sincere church-going rather than of committed faith. I should have studied theology with academic interest, but with little biblical insight. Later in my ministry I could have served people in a caring way, but I could not have led them to a living relationship with Jesus Christ, for that would have been beyond my own experience.

Life moved on, and during my years of National Service, I still looked at the Church from the outside. At that stage in my search I visualised God as some sort of Michelin X tyre man looking down from behind distant clouds – rather like Thomas Hardy's 'dreaming, dark, dumb thing, who turns the handle of this idle show'. In this state I arrived at Oxford University to begin training as a church musician. It was an escape course from the true vocation to priesthood, but at least it was looking to some extent in the right direction.

The Wistful Look

I arrived at Keble College, Oxford to study music, and soon found in the lives of other undergraduates the sort of Christian commitment and spiritual reality for which I had been searching for years. That is not to say that I had not met Christians before. Those in my home church had a notable personal faith, but it was expressed in a rather private and sacramental way, and they rather assumed that I was further on in my walk with God than was actually the case. Those whom I met in the Royal Air Force were genuine, but shy, and no one was able to help me to personal faith.

On the first day I was visited by ardent members of the Oxford Inter-Collegiate Christian Union. Eventually, I came to a vivid experience of personal conversion to Christ. The key factor was my wistful look at the lives of these students who had such glad faith and sure convictions. At first I argued hard against their testimony. They claimed to declare to me what they had 'seen and heard' to bring others into fellowship with the Father and his Son, Jesus Christ. What impressed me was the quality of their life, in terms of love and concern for others, their sense of purpose as far as the world was concerned, and their part in it. I was amazed at the way they prayed about social concerns and missionary needs abroad, as well as about personal matters like their own careers and relationships. I longed for the same reality, but found myself rebelling against their narrow views (as it seemed) on moral matters and personal behaviour. I found it hard to accept their conviction that God had spoken clearly to His world in creation, in the Bible, through Jesus Christ and through His Church. Particularly, their views about the inspiration of the Scriptures seemed hard for me to swallow.

The answer of these Christians, who quickly became my friends, was to take me to many Bible studies and sermons. Some of the finest preachers of the day were at hand, and I found a reasoned presentation of Christian truth and a strong demand to surrender all and to follow Christ. I attempted to do this after the very first sermon of term which was preached by Maurice Wood, later Bishop of Norwich. With brilliant timing he geared the end of the sermon to coincide with memorial beats of Great Tom from across the road at Christ Church, Oxford, which rang out in remembrance of those who had fallen in the two world wars. He had taken the familiar text: 'Behold I stand at the door and knock . . .' and as his fist hit the top of the pulpit in emphasis, the great bell rang out: 'Boing!' Time after time it reverberated through the building, and it made the point that Jesus Christ was outside my experience and knocking to come in, quite emphatically.

However, I was irresistibly drawn by the friendship of the Christian students at Keble who took me to endless Bible studies and prayer meetings and to multitudinous sermons and talks until the climax of my search for Christ came during a ten-day mission led by John Stott, just before the end of that first term at Oxford. On the Tuesday of the mission I decided that a solemn decision to follow with the whole of my being could no longer be deferred.

It was the moment of classic conversion experience. Room 4/112, Keble College, Oxford was my Damascus Road. The joy and sense of praise and infilling was overwhelming, and I rushed straight upstairs to my friend John Simpson to share the news. I could not be restrained: 'It's happened, it's happened, it's happened.' He cooled me down with sensible advice, and after all the years of searching sincerity, a new and personal walk with God had begun.

I no longer had to look wistfully at the lives of other Christians, but I did have to look wistfully at the life of Jesus Christ in the Gospels, longing for His standards and His beauty to be mine, as the struggle with sin and self began in earnest.

The New Look

My call to the ordained ministry came shortly after that dramatic encounter with God. Theological training followed the time at university and in June 1960 I was made deacon in the Guildford diocese. The highlight, however, came the following year when I was among the first priests to be ordained at the first ordination service in the newly dedicated Guildford Cathedral. Early years of ministry were both frustrating and yet significantly fruitful. I served for less than two years at St Paul's, Woking, only because my Vicar, Canon Geoffrey Shaw, quickly moved on to be Rector of St Leonard's-on-Sea. I joined him after a few months and we continued working together in new circumstances.

The frustration was due to the fact that I felt powerless in prayer and in ministry. I did not dry up in the pulpit as I had feared might happen, but though people were sometimes appreciative, no one seemed to be converted under my preaching, and there seemed to be little measurable success from pulpit ministry. The Holy Spirit began to move in our young people's group, as we waited upon God and sought his power and love in our lives, and we were stimulated in this quest by the experience in other churches. Young people (and their leaders too) were claiming the release of the gifts of the Holy Spirit, and were discovering a new joy in worship and prayer and a new vigour in evangelism.

The key issue at the time was that such blessing was frequently accompanied by the gift of tongues. It seemed to me that this one gift was given undue prominence, and it was spoken of as the necessary accompaniment of 'the baptism of the Holy Spirit'. This was seen as a necessary 'second blessing' in a Christian's life, as the early renewal teaching expounded the offer of Holy Spirit life and power in terms of Pentecostal theology. I could not see that the whole of one's theological framework had to be adjusted to fit a new experience of God, so my identification with charismatic realities was slow and cautious to begin with. The transformation in my life came on the road to Sussex University after I had been speaking at a parish weekend at which there were many renewed Christians. During that weekend I was finally humbled on the issue of speaking in tongues. The gift was so beautifully exercised and the contributions of different people to the meetings in words of knowledge and prophecy, were handled with such care, that I had to surrender. The key verse that spoke to me was 1 Corinthians 14:4, 'he who speaks in a tongue edifies himself.' I had judged how useful this gift was in terms of communication, and I had failed to see that through it the gracious Holy Spirit would build up my life in Christ. 'I need building up, I need edifying,' I said to God. 'Forgive me, I will not resist your working any longer.' The first jumbled words of praying and praising in tongues came during the Sunday morning Communion service. It was tentative and highly unskilled at first, but it was the beginning of a new sort of baby language expressing gurgles of love to God. At last I had become child-like enough to trust God in this matter, and I was glad because 'of such is the Kingdom of God'.

The true impact of Holy Spirit renewal came the following day. Journeying to Brighton to take part in a university mission, I realised how puny were the combined efforts of all the missioners and Christian students if we operated no better than we had in similar missions in which I had recently had a part. Then my mind turned to a verse in Paul's prayer for the Ephesians (1:19). I knew the passage well, I had studied the Greek and expounded it before university audiences. But I suddenly realised it was just head knowledge. I had never believed that 'the immeasurable greatness of his power' could be mine. I saw for the first time the sphere of operation of God's power. It is 'in us who believe'. I saw that it was resurrection power 'according to the working of his great might'.

The euphoria lasted for some weeks. It was hard to stop praising and thanking God all day long. The power and pertinence of the Scriptures have never ceased from that day to this. The new depth in counselling led to a ministry reaching thousands of people troubled by occult involvement, and this deliverance work has become a notable characteristic of our parochial work in Birmingham. Much later the experience of renewal led to deep heart searchings about inner areas of previously unrevealed resentment and anger, but in time these were dealt with. The discomfort of this inner conflict was deep and prolonged. It was infuriating to profess great joy through God's renewal, but to know a contradictory inner feeling of wrong and bitterness. I was deeply convicted by what James says about such things being 'not such as comes down from above'. He counted them 'earthly, unspiritual, devilish' (3:15), and I sought earnestly to repent and to receive afresh God's forgiveness. The release came finally with a dawning of understanding as I read 1 Peter 2:21. The writer states categorically: 'Christ also suffered for you.' That was historical and inescapable. I then realised that on the cross he accepted me long before I was even aware of my deep-rooted sins and wrong attitudes. This dawning reality in my experience was in fact the renewing work of God's Holy Spirit, dredging the murky depths of my life, and bringing some horrid things to the surface so that I could perceive them for the first time, and then deal with them. So I had to follow Christ's example by accepting myself. This was not a matter of working hard to live up to the standard of Christ so much as a matter of learning to look at myself and my failure with as much grace as Jesus does all the time. I began 'to follow in His steps' with a much lighter heart, grateful for new power in ministry, new insight into sin and inner conflict, but also new confidence in my heavenly Father as the Holy Spirit made plain the full and gracious extent of the Saviour's healing love.

The Strategic Look

My criticism of much that was going on in the Church as a result of the renewal in the late sixties and early seventies, was that it was individualistic, experiential and superficial. This was largely because the movement was sustained by rallies and conferences, drawing Christians out of their local church settings and into a hot-house atmosphere of vigorous praise and preoccupation with spiritual gifts.

Arriving as Vicar of St John's Harborne in July 1970, I had never had opportunity to work out the implications of renewal in a local church setting. This, I believed had made my life much the poorer. I should have been as strong as I might have been, strengthened, surrounded, instructed and blessed by the fellowship and support of other renewed Christians. As it was I had largely been left to my own devices, apart from belonging to a renewal prayer meeting, attached to Birmingham Cathedral. But this was made up of people who belonged to other churches. We shared a concern for Birmingham, but we did not belong to each other as members of the same local church.

At St John's, we could all work together, gladly praising

God, energetically serving God and always being in love and harmony with each other in Christ. That was the dream! The reality was utterly different. People who had prayed for change to happen in the church did not like the sort of changes that accompanied the renewal. There was fierce opposition to renewal songs and choruses. Some walked out when we prayed for God to heal the sick. Even the crowds who started attending the services caused resentment, because they took over people's favourite seats, or wore unacceptably scruffy clothing.

What should the strategy be in such a tense and wary situation? My first emphasis was to draw as many people as possible to seek God's will in prayer. More of that in the next section. Secondly I resolved to expound the strong themes of renewal – power, love, fellowship, joy etc., but without using Charismatic jargon, or language that caused unnecessary offence. For example, it was pointless for me to use the phrase 'baptism of the Holy Spirit' because all my hearers brought their own prejudices to bear on the subject before I could explain my own understanding of the subject from Scripture and experience. When I did expound its meaning, I did so using the phrase as it occurred in its New Testament context – not with all the paraphernalia of contemporary Charismatic controversy which only hindered reasonable response to what the Bible actually says on the subject. It was even controversial to preach directly on the person and work of the Holy Spirit, so we simply asked him to glorify Christ in all the preaching. During this period of sensitivity many people 'got the message' even though the headline topics of renewal were avoided. We were more concerned that lives were being changed and renewed than that a precise doctrinaire presentation was given.

Hundreds in the congregation came into a renewal experience, and many sought counselling for healing and deliverance. At that stage in the growth of the church I was still booking people in at midnight and later. As well as believing prayer and strong biblical preaching we found that to be in the centre of a parish involved in renewal required very hard work. At this time of growth and development God encouraged us by intervening with notable instances of healing. These happened at times when disagreement over change was strongest – when the choir began to break the silence whilst receiving communion by singing worship songs, or when worship dance was first expressed. The leadership did not brag about these signs and wonders, but took them as a seal on the rightness of the changes that were being introduced.

In fact change happened slowly. From the outset we were concerned to remain an ordinary parish church, with its members serving and caring in the local community, expressing loyalty within our Anglican structures. In their enthusiasm some wanted us to become more Pentecostal in style, but we were concerned that other Anglican churches, to whom we were privileged to bear testimony on choir visits and seminar days, should know that God had worked among us renewing us within a firmly Anglican, liturgical framework. In other words, what had happened among us could happen in any Church of England setting, because it depended on God working, not on the style of worship and church activity.

We looked strategically at the level of staffing. At first I believed that 'every-member ministry' meant motivating and instructing lay people to share in all the tasks of ministry and outreach, keeping full-time ordained staff or paid lay workers to the minimum. Before long it was quite clear that in a situation of rapid growth, a larger number of full-time workers was needed. It is very obvious that if a church has ten Sunday School teachers, and one is ill or cannot turn up, the vacancy can be covered by the vicar or curate. If the church grows and has forty teachers, the same percentage fall-out cannot be covered by a small professional team. Of course, there are other solutions to such a problem, but the point is made that the more a church grows, more people are needed to enable ministries to be fulfilled. Consequently after five years in the parish we jumped from two to five full-time workers.

There needed to be a strategy for growth at the practical level of finance too. I inherited a budget of some £3000 plus a year, whereas now our annual budget is rising towards £150,000. This figure includes money raised for building projects which are constantly in hand as we need to enlarge and improve our premises. It does not include a tremendous amount of generous giving by the congregation to charitable and missionary needs, in that we have a specific policy of supporting full-time workers at home or overseas through Home Groups or other groups of church members. Such giving does not appear in our accounts. To raise the level of giving as the budget increases we preach right through January on the broad theme of giving our time, our talents, our money, and ourselves. Some years we set aside two or four weeks for daily times of prayer in order to seek God's will about new ventures, and the money always comes in ahead of time in order to execute the agreed programme in an efficient way. Usually we undertake a major project over a period that is convenient for covenanting, and supplement the opportunity for pledged giving with annual gift days. The key thing is that the ministry team, which includes ordained and lay 'elders', should never have to worry about such practicalities. For several years, because of inflation, we did not achieve the fundamental aim of our regular giving. That was to have all salary and running expense costs met through the weekly envelope scheme, so that all monies given by less regular worshippers and visitors in the open plate might be given away to missionary and charitable causes.

The ministry team is vital for the ongoing work of renewal to take place. God the Holy Spirit calls people and works through people, so we needed a strategy of ministry. I looked at the needs of the area in which the church is situated with other praying people and identified the needs we could meet. We are determined only to undertake ventures that we can see through and develop, and that means that many needs are not met. We cannot do everything!

Although in Birmingham's terms, church life was strong and encouraging at St John's, many people in the parish were out of touch with God, and with our church. This was partly because the Gospel had been so vehemently proclaimed for so many years in our parish that people were frightened at the level of commitment shown by those who had responded. So they kept at a distance. Also ours is a static community in Harborne, and many people forsook the church in the aftermath of the world wars. This meant that there were many older, lonely people in the homes of our parish without any hope in Christ or knowledge of his salvation. This loneliness represents a real social problem too. For some fifteen years outreach teams have gone out from the church to care for people in their homes, daytime home groups for the retired and elderly have been established and many have found friendship and companionship and over the years some have found Christ. A large team of pastoral visitors expresses special care for the elderly, and all this work is lay led.

The core of the ministry team is an 'eldership' which first came into being in 1976. At one stage it became a source of division and hurt in the leadership, but it is a fundamental unit now for expressing loving care in counselling and healing ministries, in exercising oversight over Home Groups and their leaders, and in guiding the many who are called to train for full-time ministry in the church or missionary work abroad. The principle expressed in the early days of ministry at St John's, of working in partnership with the staff and lay people, so that they gained experience without carrying full counselling responsibility, has borne remarkable fruit over the years. It is, of course, no new idea at all, but is simply what Jesus did with the Twelve. A number of safeguards are built into our system to ensure that we work properly within the Anglican framework, particularly in not denying the PCC its full responsibility in decision making, but the measure of respect and affection in which the 'elders' are held in the congregation, is a test of their much valued ministry.

The ultimate point of looking strategically at the congregational patterns was to ensure that, as far as possible, everyone has a role and a ministry to exercise. We aim at the equipment of the saints for the work of ministry, so jobs have to be provided. We take the final commission of Jesus seriously, so evangelism is a primary concern. Over the years, hundreds have been trained and become experienced in door-to-door evangelism in the parish. Many have found their call to full-time Christian work through this enterprise. We try to limit the number of mid-week meetings for adults so that people are free either to spend time with their families (a vital priority in our strategy) or to volunteer to serve on the witness team. For example, we do not hold regular mid-week choir practices lest they should take members of the congregation out of evangelism. The main choir rehearsal is held before the Sunday evening service for this reason.

In our music-making we encourage wide participation. We use a mixed group of instrumentalists and the musical director has a rare gift of improving quite modest musical talent. Music is thus not limited to the few experts. The style is deliberately kept simple so that the whole congregation can express glad praise and worship. Some object to simple songs with repetitive words being sung. They are thought to be mindless and unfulfilling. In fact, the words are often straight from Scripture, and though simple in style the melodic lines of many renewal choruses are exceedingly well-wrought, and the musical quality stands comparison with many a traditional hymn-tune or Anglican chant. The particular blessing of this worship idiom is that at a moment's notice words that are known off by heart by everyone can suddenly be sung to provide a paean of musical praise or quiet, corporate, devotional prayer. So it was my strategy to introduce such songs. It was not just a congregational request, or some enthusiast's bright idea.

The key thing, we found, was to be careful not to introduce too much new material too quickly. To do so threatens people's feelings of security and need to 'come home' to God in worship, with well-loved liturgy and familiar music. To get new songs well known, we used them regularly at our mid-week prayer times, and because these grew to an attendance of over three hundred people at one stage, a large section of the Sunday congregation already knew and loved the music before it was introduced at Morning or Evening Prayer. Even then I taught the more difficult songs to the congregation before considering them to be part of our repertoire. Thus, no one felt excluded from the service on musical grounds. At many renewal meetings I have attended, I have been made to feel on the outside of the proceedings simply because I did not know their favourite songs. The people then seemed to be a spiritually elite group of 'in the know' Christians, who delighted themselves (and perhaps God?) with their praise, but who made the outsider feel unwelcome and unwanted. Of course, the old style of rushing through the Prayer Book liturgy without announcements or instructions to help the new worshipper had exactly the same effect.

It was this sort of attention to the small details of the dynamic of congregational life that helped to keep us together in the bonds of love in Christ. Despite the pain of new practices, because we retained familiar words from the liturgy and well-known hymns, in addition to the newer material, people eventually adjusted to new styles and freer patterns of worship. By God's grace we thus avoided a major split in thc congregation, and our testimony is one of remarkable unity and togetherness. Because new songs were added to the old, services tended to take longer, but this has not hindered the growth of the work.

The Upward and Outward Look

I inherited a weekly prayer meeting when I became Vicar of St John's. What transpired each week was as predictable as a tape recording. The prayer meeting was backward-looking rather than upward-looking to our mighty, living God of supernatural power and eternal compassion. It was clearly important to destroy that prayer meeting as soon as possible. That sounds an unloving assessment since the prayer meeting represented the devotion and faithfulness of those who had attended over many years. However, it was basically ritualistic and self-comforting. There was little selfless praise that fixed solely on the glory of God. It was a predictable hymn sandwich, during which the speaker (usually me!) filled in the allotted slot, more conscious of using up the accustomed time than conveying a pertinent message from God. All the while we looked backwards we could hardly look onwards to God's will for our future. We sought no guidance; we had no vision. We acted as a sort of false comforter to each other.

Aware of the problem represented by the traditional church prayer meeting, I had, early on the day after my institution, called together any who were concerned to find God's way ahead. This happened to be a Saturday morning, and it began a series of open praise and prayer times which we came to call 'open to God'. The title expressed all we wanted to say about our desire to be directed into God's will, indeed open to Him and His word in everything. The meeting was structured for mutual contribution and not up-front instruction. We sat in a circle so no one person dominated the gathering. It was held on the church premises and quite deliberately not in a private house, so no one felt barred from it on grounds of social distinction. Against my own tradition and instinct, I did not prepare a set talk, but attended as 'open to God' as anyone else in the group.

Some thirty or so attended early each Saturday morning, and the togetherness of this time of praise and prayer was fundamental to our growth in numbers, in ministry, and in renewal. Throughout the Acts of the Apostles St Luke records the commitment of the early Church to patterns of believing prayer – 'they lifted their voices together to God' – and we also make praise and prayer our priority. As we prayed about problem areas in the life of the church, direct answers came to us through one of the group members. Everyone came to recognise the moment when out of an awesome silence of waiting upon Him, God would speak.

One difficulty related to our programme of evangelism. I was stunned on one occasion, when after a sermon on the text, Jesus Christ, the same yesterday, today and forever, a student came up to me to disagree with what I had said. 'I did not agree with you,' he told me, 'when you said God is changing in every generation, and that the God and Father we worship today is different from the God and Father of our

Lord Jesus Christ.' That is what he 'heard' from the pulpit. It was the exact opposite of what I had said. This explained to me my predecessor, Canon Leathems's words, when he told me that no one had been converted at St John's for years. He did not understand why, since the Gospel had been faithfully preached. If some enemy was twisting the meaning of God's message, one could preach for years and not convey one word of God's truth. Clearly 'the father of lies' was at work, and we needed to discover the source of this attack on God's kingdom work.

When I took the matter to those at 'Open to God', one of our older women shared that she had experienced the same problem in communicating with an elderly lady in the parish about spiritual matters. 'I am sure it's because she has begun attending the local spiritist seance,' she shared with us. I had been quite unaware that a person within yards of our church, in a public position in the community, was one of the country's leading mediums. We felt called to bind Satan so that opposition to the Gospel might not continue, and we received a specific word from the Lord from one of our members that our evangelistic services would now always be fruitful. Since that time, some fifteen years ago, there has never been a guest service without evident conversions. Hundreds of people have come to faith in Christ through outreach visiting, personal witness, and through preaching in church. When Bishop Hugh Montefiore last preached at such a service we know of at least eight people who professed faith in Christ.

Door-to-door evangelism also proved to be a difficulty for us. Two or three people worked zealously at this task, but found no help or encouragement from the congregation at large. We waited on God to define the problems. The reason why so few shared their faith was that only one member of the congregation admitted to having friends outside the church community. We had become a separatist ghetto of like-minded believers. Our pulpit theme became, 'Make friends for God's sake.' How could we serve the community around us if we were so out of touch with it. It also became evident that so few talked to outsiders about Christ because so few spoke about spiritual matters inside the fellowship. We established two dozen home groups so that we might lose our native reserve, and become used to talking about our faith.

Seeking God's guidance at each step of our planning for 'every-member evangelism', we called out a team of witnesses from all the home groups. The evangelistic role of those who did not become part of the visiting team was to pray. The team had scores of prayer partners in a whole series of 'missionary prayer groups'. But now the mission field was that on our own doorstep. The visitors were all trained and always called in pairs, and using a simple questionnaire we asked people how we could better serve the community, as well as offering to share our faith in Christ. We acted on responses to our questions, and when the need for a playgroup was mentioned, for example, we started one which still flourishes as a bridge into the community today. We split the parish into six sections in order to visit only some 2,000 people intensively each year. This enables return visits to be made, and friendships flourish. The whole parish receives three much less intensive visitations each year by another team.

Guest services are timed to coincide with the key points of such visitations. At first, we used to organise one such service periodically, but we soon found that the new people who came to church were too far away from commitment to Christ to respond after only one sermon. However, after hearing the Gospel simply proclaimed on several successive Sundays, many would respond. Some would come to a realisation of the promises of new life and forgiveness made to them in their baptism. Some came without any Church background at all, and would subsequently be baptised and confirmed.

Many in the congregation are involved in this ongoing evangelistic venture. Some baby-sitting, some offering their homes as a base for the team, some delivering pre-visitation letters from the Vicar so that our evangelists are not confused with Mormons, Jehovah's Witnesses or Moonies. In that letter we invite any who do not wish to have us call on them to contact the church office so that we can take them off our list.

Very few ask us not to call, but the fact that we do not push ourselves aggressively on people is very much appreciated in the parish.[2] Sometimes the outreach team members are linked to home groups for prayer, and every team member has a prayer partner in the congregation. Evangelism has thus become an activity of the whole congregation and not the zealous hobby of a few enthusiasts.

As the Church has argued interminably over matters of doctrine and organisation, there has been a tremendous loss of confidence in proclaiming God's message. The world does not give up proclaiming its wares, at enormous cost in television jingles and newspaper advertisements. They put 'money where their mouth is', believing that people will be moved to purchase their goods if they shout the message loudly enough. As part of our outward look to the world, following the upward look to God, missionaries and ordained ministers have been sent out by the score from our church. Indeed, as we identify our particular calling in God's plan, the training of workers for wider ministry outside our parish is a primary vocation. The possibility of missionary service is constantly brought before the congregation, and many young people find their call to wider service in the busy work of evangelism in the parish. Parents are urged to put a priority on a strong family life in Christ, so that from their earliest days children are trained to find it natural to expect a call from God, and be available for God's service and open to any calling anywhere in the world.

Some people ask what makes us tick as a church, and what is the key note of our life. They think we swing from the chandeliers or become carried away with ecstatic hand clapping or physical jerks. None of these things would seem at all appropriate for those in our congregation who are senior professional people of high standing in the local community, even if our younger members enjoy expressing their worship in a vigorous way. The key note of our church life is obedience. Over our holy table on the east wall of our modern church building, we have a beautifully inscribed stone plaque designed by John Poole, saying 'Jesus is Lord'. We genuinely want His lordship expressed in our lives. We long to fulfil His final commission in our ministry of evangelism and missionary outreach, and so in that way, and also more obviously in the ministry of healing and deliverance, we assert His power as Lord and God over Satan's activity in the world. The experience of renewal in the Spirit brings glory to Jesus Christ, when He is enthroned in our lives as our Lord and our God. However, with that affirmed, there is always need for more and more of God's love, mercy, and grace to be manifested in us, in His Church, and in the community we serve. So Sunday by Sunday we pray "renew us by your Spirit," as we look to Him to renew even the renewal, as He fits us for His 'new heaven and new earth'.

Notes

1. See Harold Loukes, *Teenage Religion*, p. 77 (SCM Press 1963).
2. See definition of a 'parish' in the C.o.E.: Subdivision of a county having its own church and clergyman. This includes all the people in it, whether Christian or not.

NEW LIFE IN THE DIOCESE OF MOROGORO

A RURAL DIOCESE IN CENTRAL TANZANIA
The Rt Rev Gresford Chitemo

My First Contact with Renewal in the Holy Spirit

It was through Edmund John, the brother of John Sepeku, the first Archbishop of Tanzania, that I learned about renewal. As a young man he had resisted a call to serve the Lord as a priest and became a schoolmaster.

But later he was touched by the Holy Spirit and he had a vision in which the Lord laid His hand upon him, commissioning him to serve the Lord as a layman full-time to the end of his days. This meant leaving a highly respected position, in order to become a wandering evangelist. While he was studying the Bible a little later with a group of other Christians a further vision was given to him. He heard someone calling him and saying, 'Be prepared to receive a guest, and that guest is Jesus.' He responded at once, and as the Holy Spirit possessed him he came to know Jesus abiding with him and in him. From that time his life was transformed. He became at once deeply concerned for the salvation of other people. Later, he was guided to fast and pray for those who were sick, and the Lord taught him how. He would fast for three days without eating or drinking, and spend all the time in prayer and meditation. He would go to a lonely place in a nearby bush. At this place he was regularly approached by a snake, as Jesus was by Satan in the wilderness, but each time he rebuked the snake and it left him.

The clergy were deeply disturbed by Edmund John's ministry among their people, in spite of the many blessings people said they had received, so much so that they complained to the Archbishop about his brother's activities.[1]

Subsequently, a missionary from the diocese of Morogoro who attended some of his healing services told me how the Lord was healing all sorts of diseases through His servant whom people called 'Mtu wa Mungu' the 'man of God'. I went down to Dar es Salaam to see and hear him for myself. My fears and doubts that he might be one of the false prophets who the Lord said would come, quickly vanished. He was a very humble man, but firm and uncompromising. He was full of love and showed much concern for the spiritual and physical welfare of the people.

After a time in 1973 I invited Edmund John to my diocese. When he arrived we went into a parish church to pray and meditate. For the first time we learned how to fast from dawn to six o'clock in the evening. He fasted all the time. After dinner in the evening we rejoined him and continued to pray every time the hour struck. His prayers were very simple. He would say, 'Let us salute our Father.' Then he would pray, 'Almighty Father, you are full of mercy and kindness; you created the heavens and the sea and the springs of water. You, Father, created the sun, the stars, the moon and day and night. You, Father, are the creator of all things visible and invisible; and you created me as well. You created all people including those who are sick and those who are demonised. You created the whole world including wild beasts, fish, birds, elephants and all the other creatures on the earth, and the whales in the sea. You created the plains and the hills, the bushes and the trees, the fruits that are eatable and all the herbs. We thank you very much for the gift of your Son Jesus Christ to us. He is our King and the Saviour of the world. He is here with us now in all His love and power to do His work.' Then we all prayed in turn. After that we sat down in quiet meditation till the hour struck again. At that time I saw what looked like a great light going up to heaven.

For three days we prayed thus. When we came together

again on the morning of the third day I was amazed to see how the Lord had answered our prayers. As soon as we approached the door of the church we saw many people gathered there. Some of them showed manifestations of the Spirit. Some began to shake and some were crying and making a great noise. Many of them came up to the front seats where we were sitting. It was impossible to stop them from hearing the Gospel! The Lord had brought them without our invitation. They were hungry for the Lord.

Edmund John preached a very simple sermon challenging the people for coming simply to get physical healings, while the Lord had brought this ministry to them so they could hear the Gospel of Jesus Christ and be saved. Many repented and responded to the call they received from Jesus. When the time to pray for the sick came, we started with those who were demonised. It was an appalling sight. I cried as I had never cried before in pity for those who were being terribly tortured by evil spirits. Edmund John exorcised them in Jesus' Name and all of them were freed. On the second day we prayed for the sick. Some people were healed and some were not. On the third day he selected some of the pastors to pray with him. They did so, and the Lord Jesus healed many more. We learned from him by ministering alongside him and in this way Edmund John began to make this a ministry of the whole Church, and not simply that of one man. How we praise the Lord for that!

Renewal in the Diocese

Following on our time of prayer together and the ministry of healing at Berega where many people were healed in 1973, some of our pastors and lay people organised teams for fasting and prayer before ministering to the sick. As part of this ministry they called people to repent of their sins, to stop their drinking and smoking, and to accept the Lord Jesus into their lives. The Lord answered their prayers and people began to be healed here and there, and reports continued to reach me of miracles of healing taking place in various parts of the Diocese. Blind people's eyes were opened, dumb people spoke, epileptics were healed, and lepers were healed of their leprosy.

Confusion

'Beloved, do not believe every spirit, but test the spirits to see whether they are of God; for many false prophets have gone out into the world' (1 John 4:1).

Some young people started having vigils with fasting throughout the night for a three day period. Because, or so it seemed to me at the time, of their having no sleep for three days some of them began to have strange visions. One, for example, said God was calling her to go to England to preach the Gospel. She had no English and no education. She came to me and told me of the vision, and wanted a letter from me to endorse her call. In my prayers I received no confirmation from the Lord about her vision and so explained to her why I could not grant her request. Two others, a boy and a girl, came to tell me that they were shown that they should be married and that the dowry would be paid by the dioceses of Central Tanganyika and Morogoro! Again after seeking the mind of the Lord in prayer, it became clear to me that they were not moved by the Spirit of the Lord. I said no, and advised the Bishop of the diocese of Central Tanganyika to do the same. Each of these two young people in due course married other partners. Through these simple experiences we began to ask God to give us one of the revelation gifts of the Spirit referred to by St Paul, to enable us to discern true from false spirits (1 Cor. 12:10). We learned too that the deceiver can use times of tiredness caused by prolonged fasting to confuse us, and also how we may share in the spiritual warfare of children of the Kingdom. We saw the need, too, for proper oversight and leadership.

Renewal in Parishes

'How God anointed Jesus with the Holy Spirit and with power; how He went about doing good and healing all that were oppressed by the devil, for God was with Him' (Acts 10:38).

At first only a few of the pastors were filled by the Holy Spirit, and through them the people in their parishes experienced a new breath of life. The young people in many parishes responded most readily to what the Lord was doing among His people through the pouring out of His Spirit. The lives of many were not only greatly changed but the people now expected to receive both the fruit and the gifts of the Spirit to enable them to continue to share in the ministry of Jesus. They also began to expect more of their pastors.

In some parishes where the minister was unable to respond to what God was doing, those in the Renewal were critical and judgmental. As a result there was a lot of misunderstanding, and some of the renewed members of parishes were tempted to leave the Anglican Church and join some nearby Pentecostal Churches.

We met together with all the clergy to discuss the problems which sometimes followed Renewal, such as noisiness and crying and chaotic behaviour of various kinds at meetings. At our conference there was a division among the clergy to begin with, but eventually we drew up guidelines together for our people as St Paul did for the Christians in Corinth. The Lord gave us His wisdom and in our seminars many of our leaders were guided and enabled to see the difference between foolish emotionalism and obedience to God in the use of His gifts of the Spirit. They came also to see the difference between dealing with the misuse of gifts and the quenching of the Spirit by discouraging their use.

At one of our meetings those who were very rigid and proud, learned by experience when they witnessed the Holy Spirit working in power, and prayers answered, without disorder and with humility. That was a great blessing to our diocese, and slowly the disorders died out. But during the rebuking of demons there was sometimes a lot of noise, with each one shouting, but we learned to depend entirely on the power of the Holy Spirit. The majority of the clergy after a time experienced a new breath of the Spirit in their lives, and others accepted what was happening among their people.

Rubeho Parish

'While Peter was still saying this, the Holy Spirit fell on all who heard the word' (Acts 10:44).

At a Primary School in the Rubeho parish the Holy Spirit moved in great power among children gathered for worship. The Holy Spirit brought many of them under a deep conviction of sin (John 16:8–9). As they repented of their sins with weeping they also began to receive the gift of tongues. The teachers' attempts to interrupt the praise of God in tongues failed. They did not understand what was happening because they had not seen such a thing before. They reported what was happening to the school authorities who could not explain or handle what was taking place. In the end they called the local pastor and he was able to talk to the children and explain to them what had occurred.[2] As a result of this outpouring of the Holy Spirit a spiritual revival began in that area.

Many more experienced the power of the Spirit in their lives but once again the enemy also began to sow his imitations like weeds among the grain in order to bring confusion. But he was soon recognised, and once more we held seminars for our pastors and leaders to alert them to the need, not only to expect prophetic gifts through Church members, but also to submit these to testing by others who also exercise them (1 Thess. 5:21). We were learning in this way to take part in spiritual warfare and slowly there was a purification out of which beautiful charisms of the Spirit were received and the Church was built up in the Way of Salvation.

Mtega Parish

'And they came to Jesus and saw the demoniac sitting there, clothed and in his right mind, the man who had had the legion; and they were afraid' (Mark 5:15).

Because in the life of our Church we see it is now as it was in the beginning, it does not surprise us to see demons cast out by Jesus's power. Once when I visited the Mtega parish for a confirmation, I saw two girls who were quite disfigured. They were both demonised. We could not leave them in that state, so we exorcised them before their confirmation that they might increase more and more in the Holy Spirit.[3]

The following year when I was invited again for another confirmation I found these girls completely transformed. They looked quite normal and well. We praise the Lord so much for what He does for us.

Magole Parish

'Now many signs and wonders were done among the people by the hands of the apostles. And they were all together in Solomon's portico. None of the rest dared join them, but the people held them in high honour. And more than ever believers were added to the Lord, multitudes both of men and women' (Acts 5:12–14).

The people of this parish have seen the hand of the Lord doing many miracles including cripples being healed, the demonised freed, and seriously sick people healed. A paralysed man was brought on a bed made in the local fashion, and turned upside down to form a stretcher. This man was prayed for and he recovered. He carried his own stretcher and went back home. Many Moslem women have been freed of demons, and Masai people have received gifts of healing.[4] Two Masai women who were barren, asked the pastor to ask Jesus to give them children. He prayed for them and they both bore children in due course and were filled with joy. How we praise the Lord! So, as a result of preaching the

Gospel and with many signs of the Kingdom of God done by the Lord, this parish has led over four hundred Moslems to be baptised into Christ, and many Masai people also. This ministry still goes on, and we give all the glory to our Lord Jesus Christ.

It has now become the custom at every Church convention to set aside time for preaching the Gospel, and appeals are made for those who hear the preaching to respond to it. Throughout this time we will have people deep in prayer, while others minister to those who respond to the Gospel, praying with them, and for them, and laying hands upon them. God honours this work for we see many people coming into the Kingdom and released from diseases. Renewal has now permeated all parts of the diocese, and many of our young people are involved.

SOMA Conferences

At first we did not know very much about the gifts of the Spirit and how they could be used to minister to one another and within our congregations. The first time this was made clear to me and to my fellow Tanzanian leaders, was at a SOMA[5] conference for leaders held at Brokenhurst, in Kenya near Nairobi, in 1983, where Canon Michael Harper was the main speaker. Following on from that we arranged for the first Tanzania SOMA conference which was held in 1984. This was attended by most of the Church leaders of the mainline Churches which belong to the Christian Council of Tanzania. Many of them were deeply grateful to learn about the renewing work of the Holy Spirit in the Church today. Many questions they had in their minds about being filled with the Spirit, being baptised in the Spirit, speaking in tongues and the charisms of the Spirit were answered. For the first time some of them heard Christians speaking and singing joyfully and beautifully in tongues. They also witnessed ministries of healing, the casting out of demons, and other manifestations of the Holy Spirit.

At the 1984 conference, Michael Harper took the lead assisted by Jeanne, his wife, and three brethren from Kenya. The ministry was greatly blessed, and many of the leaders wanted to plan SOMA meetings in their own Churches, but we agreed to work together rather than each going his separate way. So we formed an inter-Church committee for SOMA in Tanzania. It was agreed that two dioceses should arrange Renewal conferences in Tanzania. One of the dioceses has already held a local Renewal Conference in 1986. Our second SOMA Conference was held in 1985 at Moshi. This was attended by most of the Church leaders in Tanzania, and other representatives from each of the Churches. The main speakers on this occasion were Michael Harper for the Church of England and the Rev D. Peterson, who is a Lutheran pastor from the United States. They were supported by a team from both of their countries.

God's hand was upon them in a mighty way. At one of the sessions the Holy Spirit came upon the whole conference as the speaker invoked His presence and blessing on the whole assembly. Many were moved to tears of penitence or joy as they received the power of His love.

At the same conference there were two unusual experiences with demonised people. A student in the Teachers' Training College was preaching forcefully to the people that they should repent. It was discerned meanwhile by leaders at the conference that it was counterfeit and not authentic. It was a false spirit motivating the man and not the Holy Spirit moving him (1 Cor.: 12–10). This was clearly evident when he was delivered from an oppressing spirit and set free from it. We came to understand that just as prophecy is a working of the Spirit of God, so the gift of discerning of Spirits is a work of the Holy Spirit exposing the supernatural spirits of the enemy.

The other was a young girl from Moshi town, brought to be prayed for by a relative who was a school-teacher. She seemed to be suffering from anorexia nervosa. When prayers were offered she was fierce, and abused those praying for her. Then we took her aside into a room where she remained for a time very quiet. She could not speak a word. We prayed and prayed for her, and there was no response at all. Then the Holy Spirit led us simply to sing. We started to worship by singing the chorus, 'Father we adore you . . .' To our surprise she opened her mouth and began to sing it after we had repeated it many times. We then rebuked the evil spirit and it left her. Whereas she had previously refused any food and had to be forced to eat she was now free. We took her to the dining-hall where she ate and finished a plateful and asked for more! She was at peace.

We have continued to learn about the way in which the Spirit renews congregations and heals the sick. One man whose wife attended the conference I have described was greatly inspired. Soon after, he met me and said, 'There are no lame people in our village. My wife has prayed for them and now they walk straight.' We praise the Lord.

My Ministry as a Bishop

'Jesus said, "They need not go away; you give them something to eat."' (Mt 14:16).

Through my experience of being filled with the Holy Spirit, I found a new love in my heart. This gave me a fresh concern for both the physical and spiritual welfare of people. I now have a deeper desire that all the people in my care should enjoy their physical life to the fullest extent. The diocese now has a concern to change the lives of the people of our villages and towns, both spiritually and materially.

We have organised what we call a partnership of the diocese and of the people in the parishes. In this partnership the diocese seeks funds to help the parishioners to raise their standard of life. The people of the parishes provide the land, dig over the soil and prepare it with manure and dig holes for trees, while the diocese finds seedlings of fruit trees and forest trees for them to plant. These activities demonstrate to Church members and other village people how to make the best use of the environment God has given them. They learn how to make a better use of their natural resources. We have projects to meet the needs of people where they live, by encouraging bee-keeping, and the raising of chickens, ducks, guinea fowl, rabbits, pigs, goats and cattle. We also encourage good habits of eating wholesome food, and do our best to make provision for these things. So we have places where we raise the animals and birds which they can then buy to meet their needs.

We have also provided seminar centres where we educate and train people in the use of natural resources. We praise God for the good results we have seen, as we seek to improve agricultural methods in a diocese which is mainly rural. We regard these things as part of the mission of the Church.

Health

'And He answered them, "Go and tell John what you have seen and heard; the blind receive their sight, the lame walk, lepers are cleansed, and the deaf hear, the dead are raised up, the poor have good news preached to them. And blessed is he who takes no offence at me."' (Luke 7:22).

Since the Lord has begun to reveal among us His gift of healing in our diocese, our concern for the health of the people God has called us to serve, has increased. Although we have a diocesan hospital, for which we praise the Lord, there are still many who suffer who are not able to get to hospital. Prior to my becoming involved in the Renewal Movement, I was very largely blind to the physical and mental suffering of the people we serve in the Church. I concentrated on their spiritual welfare to make sure all are saved by being converted to know Jesus Christ personally in their lives, but I had little interest in their physical needs.

Through renewal and SOMA meetings I have learned that Jesus wants to meet more than just spiritual needs. I saw that in His ministry the Lord Jesus not only preached, but healed the sick and cast out demons, and that He also gave us His power of love to grow more like Him.

Singapore and Amsterdam

'It is the Spirit that gives life, the flesh is of no avail; the words that I have spoken to you are spirit and life' (John 6:63).

'Simon Peter answered him, "Lord, to whom shall we go? You have the words of eternal life."' (John 6:68).

The Holy Spirit has given me a greater freedom to learn from and to apply the teaching that I have received. At the Institute of Advanced Leadership on Evangelism, and at the Amsterdam '83 International Conference for Itinerant Evangelists, I was greatly helped in becoming practical in the message I give, and also to expect to see results. I no longer simply take things for granted and assume there has been a response. I do, of course, pray that the Holy Spirit will give the message wings to reach the hearts of those who hear it, but now I also expect people to come forward in response to what is preached, and to confess Christ as the Lord of their lives. So now in my ministry, and in the ministries of many throughout the diocese, we make sure that all our people have accepted Jesus Christ as Lord and Saviour, and confess Him openly. Not all Church members are able yet to give such a testimony, but many are.

From attending SOMA and Renewal conferences, I have learned that Jesus not only wants all people to be saved, but also He wants them to know that they are filled with the Spirit, and to receive and use manifestations and gifts of the Spirit in their lives and ministries. There are many people now in the diocese who have received the gift of tongues, there are some who prophesy, and some who have received words of knowledge and a new and wonderful wisdom as they face problems in the Church.

The wives of the clergy are often taken for granted. They have an important place in giving support to their husbands, and so we decided to have a gathering of all the wives of the clergy in the diocese, and to teach them about the power of the Spirit of God. Some of them were transformed by the seminar and were already radiant with joy when their husbands came to join them. Then when we asked the Spirit to come and bless us all, some experienced His coming like fire and they responded by strong cryings and prayers in tongues. Others experienced a gentle touch like dew falling on them, while others felt as though His power entered their bodies from the head downwards. He deals with us as He chooses, and as He knows our need. I also experienced His power and I am glad to testify to that. It was the Lord Himself.

Unusual Confirmations

I write this having just returned from a long confirmations' safari. Of those prepared for confirmation some appear to receive the gift of the Holy Spirit at the time of prayer and laying on of hands, but it is hard to tell for others. We believe, however, that God on His side is faithful, even if some are not yet prepared to receive Him. Apart from the confirmation of the candidates we also preach sermons for all the people present at the service. At the end of the sermon an appeal is made for those who want to commit their lives to the Lord Jesus Christ. In some places where the people have been well prepared there are many decisions, and in other places few. There are places where even preaching is exceedingly hard. It is like knocking on a stone wall. At such places the responses were limited, but genuine.

On these occasions we also pray for those who need a ministry of any kind. Some want to receive a gift of the Holy Spirit for their healing. Some of these are instantly healed, and others are not healed on the spot, but receive healing some time after we leave.

On this most recent safari we had terrible cases of demons and jinni[6] which are usually single but do not easily leave those they possess. But by the grace of God, although some cases took hours, all were freed. In one case the demonised person started to throw fists at all of us, but the Lord gave us grace to be patient. There was another who was gripped by fear till he yelled and Jesus healed him. A few days later he repented very bitterly for fighting God's messengers who had come to help him. He had spent 90,000 Tanzanian shillings on doctors and medicines but these did not help him.

I now understand what it means to be a servant of the people because of Christ. Some of the ministries I have written about took us many hours. Some days we could not find time to eat. We fasted without intending to fast, because we had no time to eat. It was so with Jesus who was full of the Holy Spirit and came to be and to minister among the people. 'Then Jesus entered a house, and again a great crowd gathered, so that He and His disciples were not even able to eat' (Mark 3:20). Our hearts become very joyful when we see people come to Christ with tears of repentance, which He turns to tears of joy. We know then His heart is also filled with joy, for He seeks always for the lost, and when one is found all heaven is filled with joy too.

Notes

1. At the Lambeth Conference 1978, the editor was informed by Archbishop John Sepeku himself concerning his relationship with his brother and his testing of the authenticity of his ministry in response to questions raised by the clergy. He summoned his brother to minister in his presence. After three days and nights of fasting he began to pray for the sick. John Sepeku stood beside Edmund John and said he saw among others a child healed of blindness and another brought for healing who had died before healing could be ministered, brought to life in Edmund John's arms and handed back to the mother.
2. The Andrew Murray revival began in Wellington, Cape Province South Africa in 1860, after Murray had prayed for it every Friday for years. Young people meeting on a Sunday evening for prayer and worship in his church experienced an outpouring of the Holy Spirit. Their praise of God continued unabated in spite of the deacon's commands to be quiet. Even his

summoning of Murray himself was of no avail. He did not recognise the event he had prayed for when it happened. See *Het Lewen van Andrew Murray* by J. du Plessis pp. 204–207. Published 1920 by Uitgawe van de Zuid Afrikaanse Bijbelvereniging, Kaapstad.

3. The Apostolic Tradition of Hippolytus, quoted in *Documents of the Baptismal liturgy* by E. C. Whitaker: Published by SPCK 1960) London: Page 4 section xx para. 3 and 8. Exorcisms of candidates for baptism/confirmation performed by the bishop.
4. The Masai tribe had a reputation of being difficult to evangelise.
5. See Introduction.
6. Jinni, in Moslem demonology, are spirits lower than angels able to appear in animal or human form having supernatural powers over people.

RENEWAL AND THE FELLOWSHIP OF THE SPIRIT

ACTION AND REACTION: NEW ZEALAND
The Rev Dr Don Battley

On my way recently to a teaching conference on Signs, Wonders and Church Growth I spent a Sunday morning preaching in one of New Zealand's small rural parishes. As I stepped into the pulpit I was astonished to find a *fire extinguisher* in the pulpit! It was too good a text to ignore. 'Who put the fire extinguisher in the pulpit?' I asked. 'Did your vicar put it here in case *you* caught fire? Or have the churchwardens put it here in case *he* catches fire? Why is there a fire extinguisher in the pulpit?' After the service an amused churchwarden explained that intruders had once filled the church with powder by letting off the extinguisher so it had been hidden in the pulpit where vandals might not find it.

My mind seethed with analogies and implications. How many churches have spiritual fire extinguishers hidden away where those in authority can pull them out to douse any fire? Why is the pulpit the last place a thief would look for something explosive? Are we wanting fire in the pulpit and in the preacher? Or is it something we want to protect ourselves against?

Early Fire

New Zealanders were in fact amongst the first Anglicans to embrace the spontaneous spiritual renewal now called the

Charismatic Renewal. New Zealand priests and laity responded eagerly to the witness and teachings of both visiting teachers and indigenous Pentecostals. Guidelines were few and mistakes may have been many. Yet it was quickly evident that Anglicans could relate renewal to their own ethos without too much difficulty. Our official doctrine, especially in the Book of Common Prayer, had a clear recognition of the Holy Spirit; both the catholic and evangelical wings had maintained an expectation of grace; the healing ministry had already been planted by the catholics; and a strong tradition of worship and music was part of our heritage. Many were hungering for a more experienced faith, as theology and preaching were becoming more cerebral and more focused on societal issues. Hungry believers flocked to large conferences, key renewal parishes and to burgeoning Life in the Spirit Seminars. Furthermore, the Anglican principles of tolerance and inclusiveness coupled with a well developed balance of responsibilities between bishops and synods, and vicar and vestries allowed Anglicans the right to adopt new expressions of the traditional faith and to argue the case for it in open forums.

Reaction

This is not to suggest that the early years were easy ones. Early episcopal tolerance turned to concern as some parishes split, some clergy crashed their ministries and key renewal spokespeople increasingly expressed theologically conservative convictions. One wing of the church was particularly concerned. After some early explorations into the new phenomenon most of the newly-dominant liberal-modernists pulled sharply away, finding unpalatable the renewal's emphasis on supernatural belief, expectation of miracle and radical acceptance of the Scriptures. A generally anti-intellectual emphasis in the early renewal aggravated this separation and in reaction the more intellectually-oriented liberal leadership worked determinedly to assert an intellectual approach to the

Scriptures and a rationalistic approach to ethics. The committed charismatics, until very recently without significant institutional power, feeling besieged and frequently scandalised in conscience by the moral views endorsed by liberal-dominated synods, began to harden into beleaguered groups conscious of their minority status, anxious for their futures, dismayed at the continual discounting of their convictions and hurt at the rejection of their increasing pastoral and spiritual experience. The more the charismatics organised and pressed their witness the more they experienced social and institutional disempowerment and were reduced in their effectiveness. It is a dilemma which has taken a serious toll of the fresh vitality of the renewal. Many priests and laity have abandoned renewal life for more approved paths or have walked out of the Anglican church in anger or disappointment.

Yet through all this there have been blessings. The New Zealand charismatics have led thousands of people to new life in Christ, introducing them to the One who gives new life abundantly by the Spirit. They have received, multiplied and matured the charismatic gifts so that in any parish where they are welcomed the abilities of prophecy, healing, revelation of hidden knowledge, discernment and deliverance from evil spirits are regularly in use while the ministries of pastoring, teaching, exhorting, giving, intercession and many others are available as never before. These gifted laity urgently want priest-pastors who will recognise and utilise their ministries. Where suitably equipped priests can be found the results are excellent: the parish thrives, the mission grows and the signs of God's Kingdom are manifest. Where priests are appointed who see no value in such things, or who approve in principle but can't utilise them in practice, there can be disappointment and loss.

This is the surface picture, one that generalises from the human behaviours evident. Inevitably, this approach portrays the dynamic as one of human competition for dominance, of action and reaction, of the clash of opinion rather than a real searching for truth. But beneath it lies the deeper question of what it means to be faithful Christians today and what it means to be participants in the fellowship of the Holy Spirit.

The esteemed statement *Baptism, Eucharist and Ministry*[1] states:

> God bestows upon all baptised persons the anointing and the promise of the Holy Spirit, marks them with a seal and implants in their hearts the first instalment of their inheritance as sons and daughters of God . . . Within a fellowship of witness and service, Christians discover the full significance of the one baptism as the gift of God to all God's people.

Charismatic Anglicans would claim to have significant insights into some of the implications of this very basic New Testament concept of the fellowship of the Holy Spirit.

Origins

Most of us were nurtured to faith in 'pre-charismatic' Anglicanism. It was less demonstrative, much more reticent about spirituality, more formal and more priest-focused but with hindsight we can see the grace of God at work in our lives; we recall the sense of holiness about places, services of worship and the clergy who taught us. We were within a fellowship in which the Holy Spirit was gently present and this activity reached us with accepting love, the gift of faith and the vision of hope. It was mainly a tranquil and stable experience perhaps challenged by a stirring sermon or a life-changing decision but fundamentally it was a peaceful and well ordered life. As a theological student the sense of being bonded in the pursuit of a sacred task grew stronger even as the beginnings of protest and of search for reform began to develop. There was bonding; there was a sense of divine presence and it was fundamentally peaceful. Indeed, to fracture the peace by being argumentative or discordant was unholiness itself. Obedience to the established pattern of things was a means of maintaining the unity of the Spirit in the bond of peace. Thus were we taught in the closing stages of the pseudo-monastic model of training for ordination.

Yet even then there were stirrings. Beyond the daily round of offices and eucharists some of us sought something more nurturing and more immediate. Initially, we followed the practice of 'The Servants of Christ the King'[2] sitting in silence, invoking the presence of the Spirit and listening to the still, quiet voice. At the conclusion we felt bonded to each other and closer to Him whom we had invoked. The fellowship of the Spirit was becoming more than an institutional manifestation, more than an involvement in a sacred calling: it was becoming a personal and interpersonal reality. And again the experience was that the Spirit brought peace and a closeness between people. Most clergy and probably many laity would testify to such experiences of 'the fellowship of the Holy Spirit' both outside and within the Charismatic Renewal.

But is that what the fellowship of the Spirit is, or is there more? And might the 'more' have significantly different features to it?

Empowering

Charismatics have as their distinguishing conviction the belief and experience that when God gives His Spirit to a human being the Spirit has an empowering effect in many directions This they relate to the New Testament experience of baptism, laying claim to the expression 'Baptism in the Holy Spirit'. Debates on the subtleties of this expression were worked through in the 1970s in various books and publications. In general, Anglican charismatics do not hold to the exclusive Pentecostal view that no baptism has occurred until this spiritual encounter with its particular manifestations has been seen. They prefer to claim that, whatever early sacramental baptism may effect and sacramental confirmation reinforce, there is for every Christian one and sometimes more than one decisive reception of the Holy Spirit which will bring to fruition all that Christian baptism signifies, effecting regeneration if that has not already occurred, flooding the human heart with the divine love, opening the mind to spiritual vision and imparting spiritual abilities that are necessary for Gospel service. This is seen to be a personal Pentecost which could and probably should be more closely related to baptism and confirmation than it usually is. Certainly sacramental baptism and confirmation are seen as the descendants of the original experience of 'baptism in the Spirit'.[3] Most Anglican charismatics would see those sacraments as being in part proleptic in character, that is to say signifying and initiating that which comes to fulfilment later. The prime testimony for charismatics is not to debate the subtleties of the relationship between sacrament and experience but to affirm the reality and the necessity of a full personal Pentecost however explained or mediated.

After over a decade in this ministry I would affirm the reality of the change in people and the abiding nature of it. I have seen hundreds of believers change from being believers who assent to Christian beliefs to people who 'know that they know' the reality of the Gospel; of pew-fillers who change to ministers within a day; of listeners who become witnesses; of prayer-dry believers who become intercessors, prophets and healers. So outstanding and so beautiful is the transformation that to have to cease from ministering such an empowering would be futility indeed.

Revolutionised Vision

What this means for our understanding of 'the fellowship of the Holy Spirit' is that one's vision and experience of it is revolutionised. The fellowship of the Spirit becomes that fellowship in which the Spirit, or to be more accurate, the Father, Son and Holy Spirit, are known as the active, energising, engracing, ruling Spirit who is not just a gentle, peaceful but rather indistinct presence but is the known and ministering presence who is acknowledged as Lord.

Thus the presence is not just an idea but a known and shared reality. Therefore the fellowship of the Spirit is not simply that community of persons who receive sacraments and believe certain propositions. They are persons who recognise the Holy Spirit as a present reality, who is in each one and is active between them to bond and to energise them and to send them forth to serve. Such a statement should not be read as any denial of His presence in those who are baptised but do not claim a personal Pentecost, nor as a denial of God's presence in the world. Ultimately the subtleties of God's presence in the human race and the creation are beyond our systematising: our words, concepts and experience are too restricted to chart such a mystery. Charismatics wish simply to claim that the Christian concept of 'the fellowship of the Spirit' has at its heart the necessary recognition that the Spirit is given to be manifestly and creatively present with all the evidences that the Scriptures and much Christian history record. One of the most fundamental reasons for lifeless parishes and unadventurous dioceses is that the expectation of God's spiritual presence is negligible and that most activities are conducted at a basically humanistic level with minimal expectation of manifestations of God's power.

Although this may sound both judgmental and experience-oriented it is not meant to be so. It is rather a cry of frustration and an expression of hope. Thankfully manifestations of God's power are growing again within the Church. Renewed parishes in New Zealand have recently been introduced to the practice of calling or inviting the Holy Spirit into the midst of the congregation or prayer meeting. The result is usually a very significant increase in ministries from the congregation. Prophetic words, revelations of knowledge and anointings for healing increase. Praise and preaching become more effective. We thank God for this simple expansion of an ancient principle. The church's liturgies have opened with somewhat similar prayers for centuries and the 'epiclesis' (the calling-in of the Spirit) was central to early eucharists. An ancient truth has been given new life.

God's worship – or Ours?

The central worship of the gathered church's life should be an experience of fellowship where the Spirit, who is the blessed Trinity present to bless, is fully recognised, welcomed and invited to fulfil the purposes for which He has been sent forth. Where the Spirit comes amongst people who are regenerate and obedient to God, and are seeking to free themselves from evil, the result is an expression of the peace, love and hope of God in the midst of human beings. Out of that love-bonding can flow specific gifts of healing, encouragement and correction to those who are assembled. These may be by words anointed by the Spirit to encourage or guide an individual or the community; they may be gifts of healing given by prayer ministry during the service; or they may be gifts of insight or healing given to people in the privacy of their encounters with Him in their own hearts. However it occurs the fellowship of the Holy Spirit is that fellowship in which the Holy Spirit is present to minister fully.

This is the point at which we humans tend to reassert our control. We have designed our liturgies more to suit our wishes than God's; we define the length of our services to suit our timetables; even some of our more modern methods of caring, for example the new sciences of counselling, give the glory to ourselves. What if God wants to do it differently – to have more freedom to shape the worship, more time for intercession or ministry to persons, more direct involvement in resolving human distress so that people will forever say 'God touched me on that day,' rather than 'Reverend Smith is a very good counsellor'? When one experiences the meticulous rehearsal preceding an ordination service the question arises: 'Does God have any freedom to order this event? Has he ordered that the empowering of a minister for ordained service requires such military precision?' At what point in our worship will God be allowed rulership over the event? Or have we Anglicans learned only too well from the model of constitutional monarchy in which the monarch has only minimal powers and the government can rule without fear of intervention? When we say that the Church is the fellowship of the Holy Spirit are we saying that God by His Spirit is allowed to rule or is He asked only to bless and then only within the parameters we have prescribed in advance?

Holiness and Judgment

If there are difficulties in relation to worship they are small alongside issues of holiness and judgment. For the Spirit is the *Holy* Spirit and whatever else can be extracted from the idea of 'Holy' it is first and foremost separate, pure and belonging to God. Now if the Holy Spirit is truly acting within the Charismatic Renewal, or, to put it differently, if there is a God-inspired spiritual renewal occurring in our time, what is certain is that the holy energy so released is going to encounter the fallenness and disobedience of the world and that the encounter will be vigorous and costly. It is just here that widespread naïveté has confused us all. A lot of people, charismatics and not, have had the thought that we could have genuine church renewal with a lot of peace and healing and praise. It has been a general assumption that a truly charismatic renewal will produce a nicer, sweeter, more loving and more united church. Therefore, where there have been conflicts the assumption has been 'someone has blundered'. Obviously this is an oversimplification to make a point. Although we live under Paul's injunction, 'In so far as it lies with you, live at peace with all,' the reality of the situation is that the Holy Spirit is the Spirit of the One who said:

> Do not think that I have come to bring peace on earth; I have not come to bring peace, but a sword. For I have come to set a man against his father, and a daughter against her mother . . . and a man's foes will be those of his own household (Matt. 10: 34–36).

Any superficial reading of the Gospels and Acts shows Jesus and the apostles being greatly involved in conflict, for they were confronting all the bondages of the human race: unbelief, demonisation, guilt and sin, institutionalised power, superstition, spiritism, decayed religion and formalised belief systems. They couldn't move without running into trouble! And who sent them into it? The Holy Spirit sent them into it. They were on the front line of the conflict of powers holy and unholy, serving a Kingdom of holy power which was coming forcefully. The most likely meaning of Matthew 11:12 is simply:

> From the days of John the Baptist until now the Kingdom of God has been coming forcefully and men of violence attack it.

Confronting the Church

In the light of this sort of principle the hope of some charismatics for an casy welcome to a new return of kingdom-power is naïve and the wish of church leaders that spiritual renewal could behave itself nicely and not cause too much trouble is similarly unreal. Because the truth is that we are not in the business of maintaining a happy pool of serenity and good middle-class behaviour. We are in a grave and serious conflict in a sin-sick world. We have, of course, more than enough grounds for trying to avoid religiously-inspired conflict. Both Ireland and Lebanon are tragic warnings of the genocidal nature of religious conflict. The search for peaceful solutions in a world poisoned by violence is a high imperative. Yet spiritual conflict is real and at times beyond our preventing because it arises in the spiritual realms.

What we can too easily miss in our scriptural heritage is that much of the conflict portrayed there was *within* the Israel of God. Thus Matthew 11:12 relates to the conflict between John the Baptist, the servant of the Kingdom, and Herod Antipas, the half-Jew who was seen by many as a traitor to the calling of the nation. We too easily forget that when the Holy Spirit comes to a fallen or compromised Church He comes as prophet and, if need be, as accuser. Ahab's fearful response to the arrival of Elijah 'Have you found me, O my enemy?' (1 Kgs. 21:20) may well be the response of an apostate church to a visitation of the prophetic Spirit.

The deeply troubling experience of charismatics is just how much sheer spiritual bondage is present today within the Church. Both clergy and laity are frequently found to be bound by sinful behaviours or held by various forms of spiritism, witchcraft or ancestral spirits. Many men are blinded spiritually by the serious spiritual bondage of freemasonry;[4] fears and compulsion rule the lives of very many Christians while the very forms of religion, no matter how hallowed or piously designed in the past, can become bondages on the lives of their faithful servants if the externals become substitutes for the inner reality. Although there have been many noble and creative developments within modern institutional Anglicanism that, albeit with some reservations, can be received as real manifestations of God's Kingdom at work, big questions remain for many charismatics on the soundness of the modern Church's faith, its understanding of Christian ethics, its spiritual discernment, its selection of persons for ordained ministry and even its perception of its mission in the modern world.

Amidst such an admixture of true regeneration, worldly Christians and moral and theological pluralism, the Anglican charismatic confronts a number of dilemmas: to speak plainly and stir up fights; to work in the privacy of the parish trying to build a cleansed community (but even there the issues are right in front of them); to stand openly for the spiritual issues risking official disapproval and allegations of narrowmindedness and judgmentalism. Anglican charismatics at least in the Western churches tread a narrow line between trying to maintain the unity of the Spirit with all believers and needing to draw the attention of the Church to its urgent need for deliverance on so many fronts.

All this is included in experiencing the fellowship of the Spirit. At times it is unity, peace and joy in the Holy Spirit; at times it is tension and embarrassment in the midst of a compromised church; sometimes it is confrontation over fundamental issues. When such confrontation occurs the charismatics all too often lose out either through lack of experience or lack of numbers. But that does nothing to reduce their concern about church leaders or synods that seem to sit lightly to such serious spiritual issues.

Ecumenical Dimensions

The ecumenical implications of the Charismatic Renewal are particularly paradoxical. Charismatics experience a very strong sense of transdenominational unity based on the common experience of the Spirit. I recall the amazement and joy of a New Zealand Pentecostal pastor, a former Church of Ireland member, who on visiting his homeland sought to find a Catholic charismatic prayer meeting. Finding himself lost on the way he stopped his car to ask a Catholic nun if she knew where it was. 'Just follow me,' she cheerily replied. He soon found himself amongst a community of Christians who worshipped the risen Christ with fervour and joy, using tongues and prophecy and scripture exposition. 'I felt I had truly come home,' the pastor declared. 'All my enmity and mistrust melted away. These were my sisters and brothers and I rejoiced to see such things in my own land. I can never preach against Catholicism again.'

The contribution of such experiences to the ecumenical journey cannot be overestimated. The proverbial grassroots are being granted a foretaste of the vision of the Church reunited. Charismatics like to claim 'this is the true ecumenism'. But there are difficulties with this view because it is a unity expressed in a new church culture which in many ways tries to bypass the inherited traditions of the churches. In that Pentecostalism is very much a twentieth-century phenomenon (even if its roots do lie further back) then the ecumenism of the charismatics is flawed by its attempt to step out of the past into the new present. It is not that the spiritual unity is untrue – for it is the One Spirit who blesses and inspires – but culturally the charismatics are in danger of trying to shortcut the massive problems of history and in the long run this cannot succeed. Yet the contribution of charismatic experience to ecumenism could be considerable because it creates not only a highly energised basis for recognition of each other as full Christians but also a climate of impatience for resolution of the historical difficulties.

Unfortunately, it has also to be faced that the charismatics are themselves an ecumenical problem. They have added a further church culture to the historical churches and have given rise to new tensions, new rigidities of thought and renewed cross-polemics within the churches. The widespread antipathy and tactics of exclusion displayed within those churches towards the charismatics threatens to compound a potentially difficult situation. Because the charismatics are a further ecumenical issue which ecumenical leaders must attend to, it certainly does not help when delegations (such as the New Zealand one) to the Vancouver meeting of the World Council of Churches included representatives of every recognised minority in the church, but not one charismatic leader. Such discrimination only distances charismatics from the formal ecumenical process.

A further ecumenical issue is the evident hostility of some liberal church leaders towards Pentecostals.[5] In New Zealand some Anglican leaders have been speaking out against the dangers of 'sectarianism' alleging anti-intellectualism, racism, sexism, judgmentalism and fundamentalism as dangerous faults. The concerns may be real enough but the attacks are markedly inconsistent with sound ecumenical principles. The impression is given that there are two types of other churches: approved ones to be related to ecumenically, and disapproved ones to be openly criticised. Charismatics are dismayed and embarrassed to read about such intolerance towards Christians whom they have good reason to love and may wonder whether they are also perceived to be unwanted 'sectarians'. If so, then the ecumenical task exists within the Anglican Church as well as outside it. Anglican leaders need to reflect upon the lengthy history of church-versus-chapel antagonism and to be careful not to reactivate it. In many independent Christian fellowships those painful memories are just beneath the surface, and resurrecting the old charge of sectarianism will help no one.

Peace or Division

Living in the fellowship of the Spirit therefore proves to be a bittersweet and paradoxical experience for all Christians especially in times of pluralism and rapid change. As Anglicanism diversifies throughout the world and embraces a variety of new movements, increasing discernment will be necessary. Not all the issues can be resolved by dialogue and compromise. Points will arise where the issue will be, 'What accord has Christ with Belial?' (2 Cor. 6:15). The big problem is deciding *what* is Belial ('of the evil one'). For charismatics Belial includes unbelief, immorality and forbidden spiritualities. For others the measure is more humanistic. In the de-spiritualised world of modern rationalism, spirits have negligible reality. For charismatics such a view is blindness indeed.

There is therefore the real possibility that the coming of the gift of the Spirit in power could lead not to peace and harmony in the Body of Christ but to conflict and division. By and large charismatic Anglicans seek to avoid confrontation for both political and spiritual reasons. Yet there is an inexorable logic to the proposition that when the Holy Spirit comes he comes as a purifying fire not just to the world (John 16:8–11) but also to the Church (Luke 3:16–17). There is a long history of visitations of the Holy Spirit producing schism in Israel at the same time as He leaps over established barriers to fellowship. Most charismatics have stood in the shoes of Peter going to Cornelius' house and of Stephen facing his accusers within the community of faith.

Charismatics cannot avoid being challengers of two major emphases in the modern church: traditionalism and liberal radicalism. For the traditionalist the charismatic is an irreverent innovator who overthrows the treasured peacefulness of the church and promotes the apparent non-sense of tongues, prophecy, miracles and unstructured worship. For the radical, the charismatic is a credulous believer trying to return the Church to primitivistic believing. All three groups live uneasily with each other in the church: in a voting situation any two can usually prevent the third imposing their will yet, despite there being generous amounts of Christian forbearance operating between them, none of them really trusts the other. There is in fact a very serious struggle being waged within the Church as to which view will determine the future shape of the Church, and a satisfactory outcome is by no means assured. What is very apparent in New Zealand is that the liberal-radical wing hold a lot of institutional power but have limited grassroots support while the charismatics are in a reverse position. The present trend is for electoral synods to choose mediators as bishops – men of sufficient breadth to appreciate the gifts of each sector.

This is no new role for bishops. Current New Testament scholarship indicates that the diversity within the apostolic Church was probably even wider than in our own time and that the second-century episcopate emerged to manage the problems of diversity. As Anglicanism has cut loose from its earlier definitions of belief and worship it has opened itself to new diversities. The creative management of these will be the key to its corporate effectiveness for the next generation or more.

It is to be hoped that the solution sought is not merely to soften the edges and to dampen the conflict. Some of the issues are too serious for such a humanistic solution. It is time the key issues were faced more openly including the just sharing of opportunities in leadership. Charismatics ask for a full share in the leadership of the Church. They have witnessed and served faithfully to their experience of God for some twenty-five years. They still live in the hope that the Spirit who reformed them into apostolic believers will similarly renew the whole Church bringing forth new manifestations of what it really means to be the fellowship created and sustained by the Holy Spirit. They look increasingly to the episcopal leaders of the Church for recognition of the validity of their concerns, the maturity of their experience and the costliness of their faithfulness to the fellowship of the Holy Spirit.

Notes

1. World Council of Churches, *Baptism, Eucharist and Ministry*, Paragraphs 5 and 10, Geneva: World Council of Churches, 1982.
2. The Servants of Christ the King were a fellowship of praying Anglicans formed in England during World War II who practised 'waiting on the Spirit'. See Olive Parker, *The New Commandment: the Servants of Christ the King*, (DLT 1962).
3. Probably the most helpful scholarly consideration of this issue is James D. G. Dunn, *Baptism in the Holy Spirit* pp. 224–9 (SCM 1970).
4. Charismatics consistently find that men who have made the vows of freemasonry need to renounce the power of those vows and to be delivered from the dark forces associated with them before they can receive the gifts of the Holy Spirit fully.
5. For convenience, I use 'Pentecostal' to indicate the Pentecostal churches and 'Charismatic' to refer to the charismatics in the historical or 'mainline' churches.

THE PARABLE OF THE DURIAN TREE

THE LORD AT WORK IN SINGAPORE
The Rt Rev Moses Tay

The apparent insignificance of Singapore was brought home to me recently in one of my overseas trips. I was asked by a number of people: 'Where is Singapore? Is it in China? Is it part of Japan?' I referred them to a world map. 'Somewhere between Asia and Australia', I said, 'you will find a group of islands near the equator. Look for a peninsula called Malaysia just north of the equator; Singapore is the dot at the southern tip.'

The tiny island Republic of Singapore with a land area of 600 square kilometres, a population of 2.6 million people and a stable government, but without natural resources, is an economic miracle, in spite of the recent recession. More than that, we are seeing the beginning of a divine miracle as the Lord touches it to fulfil His purposes.

The story of renewal in the diocese of Singapore has been told by various people in different ways. It is not my intention to attempt to produce an authorised version or a revised standard version of the history of renewal on this island, but simply to highlight some salient features of what has begun to happen as we move on with our God.

In 1972, some students of one of our Anglican secondary schools, St Andrew's School, were hungry for God. As they prayed together one night on a field, the Holy Spirit fell upon them. They were touched with the reality of God and spoke with tongues. They were so overwhelmed with joy that some of them could not take their geography test the following day! In the same year, a similar event occurred among students of a Methodist Secondary School in Singapore, as well as with students in Kuching in East Malaysia. In retrospect, we see this as a sovereign move of the Holy Spirit.

The Leadership

My predecessor, Bishop Chiu, was baptised soon thereafter in the Holy Spirit, as he has related in the book, *Bishop's Move*.[1] Since then most of our clergy and many of our lay people have experienced baptism in the Holy Spirit. Some of the clergy experienced spiritual renewal outside Singapore, but many more under the tireless and faithful ministry of Bishop Chiu.

It cannot be too strongly stressed that clear and courageous leadership is crucial in renewal. The Lord has moved, and we must move with Him. For the bishop there is always the nagging fear of division, for he is a focus of unity. But unity in Christ is a unity of the Spirit. It is a given unity. We cannot create it, but we are to maintain it (Eph. 4:2–3). The Holy Spirit does not bring division but division is often a result of the Spirit's working. Any division relating to the exercise of the gifts of the Spirit may be caused by deviations or excesses, often from over-enthusiasm. Even more frequently it is caused by the quenching and restricting of the Holy Spirit by a leadership which is unwilling to risk itself in submission to the Spirit of God, who blows where and how He may choose. The leadership of the Church has a mandatory responsibility to teach about, and to guard and guide the manifestation of the gifts of the Holy Spirit in the Church.

Personal Pilgrimage

I was born and bred in an Anglican family, and worshipped at St Andrew's Cathedral in Singapore regularly during my undergraduate years. After graduating in medicine in 1962, I worked in the General Hospital in Malacca, Malaysia, where

I had previously received my secondary school education. One Sunday afternoon, after I returned from the wards to my room in the hospital quarters, the Lord began to speak to me and urged me to go and share the Gospel with the patient in bed three Ward D1. I resisted. How could I take advantage of my patient, a poor victim, and ram my personal faith down his throat? The Holy Spirit persisted: 'If I say to the wicked, "You shall surely die," and you give him no warning, nor speak to warn the wicked from his wicked way, in order to save his life, that wicked man shall die in his iniquity, but his blood I will require at your hand' (Ezek. 3:18). After much struggle and protest I finally went back to the ward. The patient had heard about Jesus while he was at a Catholic school. After a brief talk with him I led him in a prayer to receive Jesus into his life. Then I left quickly, wondering whether the patient had really been saved.

The next morning during the ward round, I noticed that the patient looked happier and brighter, but on the third day he died. The reality of life and death hit me, and especially the joy of eternal life, and the looming darkness of death without it.

Soon afterwards I left the hospital to start private general practice in Muar, a town some forty-five kilometres from Malacca. This was not of my own choice but because of family circumstances and, in retrospect, of divine providence. It was during these seven years of medical oblivion, a wilderness experience, that I began to learn the ways of God. I had the opportunity and joy of helping with two youth groups of the two Presbyterian congregations in Muar, but in the process, I was 'trained' unknowingly by the young people in practical ministry for the Lord. One of the youth groups has since developed into a full-grown congregation, led today by a Spirit-filled pastor.

At a conference in 1964 which I had a hand in organising, I firmly committed myself to serve God in any capacity, including full-time missionary work. The prevailing circumstances seemed to make the latter impossible, but the Lord spoke to me in the words of 1 Corinthians 2:9–10: 'But, as it is written,

"What no eye has seen, nor ear heard, nor the heart of man conceived, what God has prepared for those who love him," God has revealed to us through the Spirit.' These words strengthened me. I studied His Word systematically and worked for a degree in Theology (B.D.) while practising medicine and helping in the Church. In the fullness of time, and in the midst of distracting challenges, the Lord directed me in 1970 to return to Singapore. He did so with words from Isaiah 30:18–26, in which He outlined for me His promises and expectations.

I was on the verge of leaving medical practice for full-time ministry, but that was not to be for a while. I joined the Ministry of Health as a medical officer. For a time I 'floated', preaching at various churches at their invitation, until one Sunday, my wife and I strayed back to St Andrew's Cathedral. The Cathedral where I had worshipped during the late 1950s had become a new place. The liturgy was basically the same but the preaching was different. The presence of the Holy Spirit in the preaching was almost tangible. We decided to stay. I soon became a lay reader, and was much encouraged by Canon Frank Lomax in my preaching and teaching ministry.

Personal Renewal

For some time I was involved mostly in Sunday activities and so was shielded from the winds of renewal that were blowing through the diocese. My first experience of a charismatic meeting was at the dedication prayer-meeting for the month-long Diocesan Mission led by the Rev Trevor Dearing during his first visit to Singapore. For the first time I heard people speaking in tongues with interpretation and prophecy, and saw many 'slain in the Spirit'. The whole atmosphere was electrifying, if not somewhat eerie to me. I left the meeting with a sense of wanting never again to become involved in a similar gathering.

But that brief experience could not be shelved. The burning

question in me was: 'Is this a work of God or is it not?' If it was not the work of the Holy Spirit, I should not simply stay away and keep quiet about it. But if it really was His work, then I wanted to be drenched in the Spirit. I searched the Scriptures intensely concerning the gifts of the Holy Spirit. I concluded that there was nothing contrary to the Word of God in what I had seen and heard, but rather that the Scriptures had been fulfilled before my very eyes.

During the concluding days of the Mission at the Cathedral, my wife and I at last decided to attend the meetings. We were so busy bringing sick friends to these meetings that we had not gone forward to receive ministry ourselves. It became clear that we should not fail to receive ourselves so great a gift from God as His own Spirit, and so when the invitation for those seeking Baptism in the Holy Spirit was given, we moved forward at once. What a flood of people there was! The sanctuary was so packed with people that it was not possible for them to be prayed for with the laying on of hands. All the same the Holy Spirit came upon us. The exhilaration of joy and the intense awareness of the presence of the Lord lifted me up on high for several days.

For some time I did not receive the gift of tongues although I knew about the gifts of the Spirit listed in 1 Corinthians 12. To me, 'Do all speak in tongues?' implied that not all needed to speak in tongues. One day, however, my brother told me that tongues as a language of prayer and praise is available to every Christian. Paul, who would rather speak five intelligible words to instruct others than ten thousand in a tongue, claimed that he spoke in tongues more than all the noisy tongue-speaking Corinthians (1 Cor. 14:18–19). I came to understand that speaking in tongues is not only for my edification, but may also be used as a prophetic gift in the Spirit, when Christians are gathered together and the utterance in tongues is interpreted by someone who is present. Praying in tongues, on the other hand is a 'heart to heart' expression of the inexpressible wonder of our relationship with the Father in Jesus Christ. It is prayer in the Spirit in the context of our fellowship with God in the Holy Trinity (1 John

1:3). How could I then not ask for so great a gift? And so I asked the Lord for this blessing and spoke out in a tongue. At the same time His Word to me was, 'You have been changed.' This happened on my birthday. What a birthday present that was!

One of the early results of my being baptised in the Holy Spirit was that I began to find serving the Lord exciting. Almost immediately after the Diocesan Mission with Trevor Dearing, I left for Bangkok to attend a course for a month. During this time I was able to hear the Lord more clearly for daily living and for sharing the Gospel with others. I was led unexpectedly to share in two Thai churches about how the Spirit of the Lord was moving in power among His people in Singapore. It was a joy to see scores of Thais coming forward to give their lives to the Lord, to be filled with the Holy Spirit, and to receive other blessings from God.

Another result of being baptised in the Spirit was that I received a new freedom in sharing the faith with others and became more effective in doing so. One day a young man whom I did not know called me and asked for an appointment to discuss a complicated personal problem. We met as agreed. As he began to talk, the Holy Spirit made it clear to me that what he really wanted was to receive Christ. So I interrupted him and asked him if he wanted to receive Christ into his life. He replied positively and eagerly, and after a brief explanation I led him to yield his life to the Lord. His problem, which I had not dealt with, faded at once into the background.

The most important result of my being filled with the Holy Spirit, was that I entered the ordained ministry on a non-stipendiary basis, with the encouragement of Bishop Chiu. Very soon I was given the oversight of a new congregation while I continued to be a Director of a government hospital. Ministering in the power of the Holy Spirit opened up wholly fresh spiritual dimensions and was a deeply satisfying and maturing experience. What was more, people who had been closed to the gospel were now responding to Christ, frequently through prayers for healing and deliverance.

In 1982 I was elected Bishop of Singapore to succeed

Bishop Chiu. At his farewell service in August 1982, Bishop Chiu shared with the people what I had shared earlier at a clergy meeting concerning my own pilgrimage and call. In particular he read the words from Isaiah 30; 18–26 which had given a new direction to my life, and confirmed these as the Lord's words both to me and to the diocese.

A few days after Bishop Chiu left for England, my wife had a subarachnoid haemorrhage due to a congenital aneurysm of an artery at the base of the brain. She recovered the following day but an early operation to clip the aneurysm was advised. After the operation she lapsed into a coma and was put on the respirator. It was a difficult and, indeed, a poignant and painful time for me, but the grace of God was sufficient in my weakness, and He manifested in this sad event His own triumphant Spirit at every turn. The clergy and people of the diocese rallied around us and prayed for us. Some were given remarkable visions of our needs and came to pray and minister to us. Never was a diocese so united in prayer for a bishop-elect! Never was there a bishop-elect who had such evidence of the love and gifts in ministry of his clergy, or a more encouraging glimpse into the hearts of his people! Thus the Lord welded us into a deeply intimate fellowship which is in itself a sign and an expression of the Kingdom of God. This becomes possible as the bishop, the priests and the people become a body owned by the Spirit of the living God.

After a week on the respirator, my wife went to be with the Lord. This was two months before my consecration. Within two and a half years the Lord graciously gave me a new companion to share my life. She too is a delightful, gentle and gifted lady.

Effects of Renewal

A report of a two-year study on the effects of renewal, begun before Bishop Chiu retired, was presented at the Diocesan Synod in May 1984. Basic questions were raised in the study. What is the main purpose of the Church? How has renewal in the Holy Spirit affected the life and mission of the Church? The report was written in the format of a medical research paper using standard statistical methods with the aid of a computer.

The Great Commission as described in the Acts of the Apostles was used as a yardstick for measuring the effects of renewal: 'But you shall receive power when the Holy Spirit has come upon you; and you shall be my witnesses in Jerusalem, and in all Judea and Samaria and to the end of the earth' (Acts 1:8). The study established the reliable indices for measuring the 'output' of the Church in terms of church growth and mission. It then evaluated about ten 'input factors', as common activities characteristic of traditional and renewed congregations in the diocese, to see if they were statistically significant in contributing towards the 'output score', namely, a measurement for the fulfilment of the Great Commission in terms of church growth and mission.

The only four input factors that were statistically significant in contribution towards the 'output score' were:

1. The use of free worship on Sundays
2. Charismatic vicar or priest in charge
3. Prayer and Praise meetings
4. Life in the Spirit Saints Alive Seminars

On the basis of these four factors, which were distinctive of Charismatic Renewal, the study defined the charismatic index i.e. the degree of renewal for each congregation. It then evaluated the relationship between the charismatic index and the 'output score'. Analysis of the four 'input factors' and 'output scores' was also performed.

The study showed that:

1. All the factors associated with a high output score were found only in the Charismatic Renewal.
2. All the factors distinctive of the Charismatic Renewal studied were associated with high output scores.
3. There was a very significant correlation between the charismatic index and a high output score.

It was concluded that Charismatic Renewal had a profound and beneficial result in the Diocese of Singapore.

Subsequent statistics merely confirmed the findings of the study. For example, data on confirmations showed that during the decade prior to renewal (1963–73), the total number confirmed was 2,282, an average of 228 a year. For the decade of renewal (1973–82), the total number confirmed was 4,954, an average of 495 a year. This is an increase of 117%. The figures for 1983, 1984 and 1985 were 781, 924 and 1,043 respectively.

The overall effects of renewal include the reality of the presence and power of God in individuals and in our corporate life, and an urgency to reach out with the love of God in mission and power evangelism. These are accompanied by the 'conversion of purses' so that tithing and sacrificial giving become the norm of Christian giving.

Renewal and Decision Making

Renewal in the Spirit, accompanied by a fresh realisation of the Lordship of Christ, invariably has a profound effect on how the Church is run. In the making of decisions some of our parishes have moved away from the tradition of a majority vote, to reaching a consensus or requiring unanimity. The basis of this change is simply that if every member seeks and discovers the mind of the Lord, all will arrive at the same decision. Whenever this happens there is much blessing and growth.

In many parishes our clergy take their lay-leaders for retreats from time to time, in order to pray together, minister to one another, and to seek the mind of the Lord for His people. The parishes are then encouraged to pray and to crystallise the vision and goals He gives each congregation and to share these at our Synod in November of each year. The Diocesan Boards are encouraged to do the same. Because Singapore is so small and compact we take advantage of our weekly clergy meetings to pray and to share and so to learn to move together in obedience to the Lord.

Renewal and Structures

The diocese continues to function under the same constitution as before, with its Synod, Standing Committee and eight Diocesan Boards. Spiritual goals and dimensions have, however, been infused into many of these meetings as a consequence of personal renewal.

Each parish continues to function under the Vicar, the Parochial Church Council, with, in addition, full-time parish workers licensed by the Bishop and financed by the parish. Each parish is considered as a functional unit and is structured into three levels for growth:

1. Primary Groups or Home Cell Groups, with eight to sixteen people meeting in homes during weekdays for prayer, Bible study, evangelism, caring, sharing and mutual ministry. The focus is on personal involvement.
2. Secondary groups, e.g. Choir, Servers, Youth Fellowship, Young Adults Fellowship, Women's Fellowship, each with fifteen to fifty people. The focus is on activities in common towards a common objective.
3. Tertiary groups, e.g. Church services, evangelistic outreach with as many people present as possible. The focus is on the community event or celebration.

In the development of the parish, especially in the Primary Groups, the emphasis is on the building of the people of God. Each person who attends any of the services or activities is nurtured in terms of personal spiritual development, comparable to career development in the secular world. Each person is taken through the basics of the Christian faith and victorious Christian living at baptism and confirmation classes. After confirmation, each member is then trained and equipped for service in general and also in specific areas.

Ministry of Lay People

The Lord has shown us that one of the keys for fulfilling the mission of the Church is the freedom and encouragement of lay people in the exercising of their ministries. It is the whole people of God who are 'a chosen race, a royal priesthood, a holy nation, God's own people' (1 Pet. 2:9). Gifts of the Holy Spirit are given to members of the Body of Christ and not simply to those who are ordained (1 Cor. 12). If gifts of the Spirit are being manifested among the laity, as a lively reality as indeed they are, the Lord must mean them to exercise this ministry within the liturgical framework of congregational life, as well as in the world outside.

There has been a radical change in the pattern of the one-man-one-congregation, where the Vicar or Priest in Charge has often been the bottle-neck and sometimes the cork. We have encouraged some lay people who are evidently exercising ministry gifts to become full-time parish workers. At the start, theological qualifications or training were not specified, but we now require qualifications with continuous upgrading based on our Diocesan lay training scheme. The number of licensed parish workers has increased steadily during the last four years. About half of them are women, and just over one third have received a full theological training.

The training of our lay people has become an urgent priority. Our goal is to train, equip, and mobilise every member to serve the Lord. The time-honoured manpower projections or theological education by extension, are quite inappropriate and inadequate where the Spirit of the Lord is moving in power. The training has to be directly relevant, immediately useful, easily available and attainable, while those being trained continue to fulfil their role in the Church.

In our Diocesan lay-training programme, we focus on three basic areas. Namely, practical ministry, including the exercise of the gifts of the Spirit; the Word of God; and personal growth in maturity in the Christian life. The training programme is thus divided into three parts called for convenience year one, year two and year three. Anyone who has been confirmed may begin with any subject in any year.

In year one the focus is on practical ministry based on the twenty 'How to' modules (see Appendix). Each module consists of ten lessons, and requires ten sessions, normally conducted for a period of ten weeks in the parishes, but co-ordinated at the Diocesan Office. A certificate is issued for each module completed. At the time of writing, 3,500 have been awarded. On the completion of any ten modules, a certificate of lay ministry is given.

In year two the aim is to give each person a working knowledge of the Scriptures. The scheme consists of twelve units to cover the Bible, with additional introductory and theme units. This is basically a self-study course requiring ten weeks for each unit. Guides to each unit and tutorial sessions are available to help students prepare for an examination at the end of each ten-week period. A certificate of biblical studies is awarded for successful candidates on the completion of ten units.

In year three the focus is on character and training, primarily in discipleship and leadership. Fifteen units have been mapped out. Some of these units require residential training and involvement in specific projects. On completion of ten units a certificate of church ministry is awarded.

On the completion of the entire three-year programme, a Diploma of Ministry will be awarded. Our lay training programme is shared with the Diocese of Sabah, and the training materials are available to any person on request.

A separate scheme for training in children's ministry is being developed for Sunday School teachers, and others teaching and ministering to children. Anyone wishing to teach Sunday School is required to work through four basic units, and all Sunday School teachers are encouraged to persevere with training in special areas. The emphasis is not merely on teaching, but also on ministering to children. So far about 150 of our Sunday School teachers have attended the basic course.

Home Cell Groups

A significant key to growth has been the development of Home Cell Groups. Our Lord Himself has promised His own presence where two or three are gathered in His name. It is the small groups like these within our parish structures, which have flourished in the most adverse circumstances, and both in early Church history, and in our own time, have survived in times of persecution. But what is quite as important is that they are a means by which the people of God are built up in a mature Christian life.

While our trained lay people are equipped to bear witness to Christ in any situation, it is in the Home Cell Groups that they are able to put their training into use most effectively. We encourage every member of a congregation to belong to one of these groups, which normally meet once a week. The leaders and assistant leaders are all trained and appointed by the Vicar or Priest in Charge and it is expected that each group will divide when its numbers exceed fifteen or sixteen. Many of the Home Cell Groups have become splendid growth points for the Church and the most effective agents for evangelism. But initiation into the Body of Christ must be followed by growth in discipleship, and to this end groups are used for the study of the scriptures, prayer, and for a ministry to one another. We have hundreds of Cell Groups in the diocese, but many more are required to meet the needs of our people.

Ministry of Women

Where do the women come in? Almost everywhere. In addition to the more traditional role of women in the Church, we have women leading worship, leading Home Cell Groups, in teaching, in prophecy, in deliverance ministries, and no one raises an eyebrow. But the ordination of women is another question!

We believe we ought to return to Scripture and master the divine arithmetic of 1 plus 1 = 1 as given in Genesis 2:24, where we read, 'Therefore a man leaves his father and his mother and cleaves to his wife, and they become one flesh.' For too long the Church has sought to use only half of God's creation in the ministry. Now the Church wants to use the other half, with women in the ordained ministry. It is our experience that where a clergyman has a wife also committed to the Lord and in His service, we find a parish is greatly blessed. I am more and more convinced that we cannot be satisfied with second best. I continue to look for faithful couples before I ordain a man to the priesthood. This does not mean, of course, that I will not ordain unmarried men, but that I recognise the married state as the usual condition for men and women. Where couples are called by the Lord into His service, the problem of the ordination of women does not arise, and we can hear St Paul without contortions when he says, 'I want you to understand that the head of every man is Christ, the head of a woman is her husband, and the head of Christ is God' (1 Cor. 11:3). Is it a wonder that the ordination of women is so thorny and divisive an issue? Is it not logical to conclude that where Church leaders are sharply divided on such an issue the mind of God is not being discerned? 'But the wisdom from above is first pure, then peaceable, gentle, open to reason, full of mercy and good fruits, without uncertainty, or insincerity' (Jas. 3:17). The opposite of heavenly wisdom is 'earthly, unspiritual, devilish' (Jas. 3:15). Are we not appalled?

Power Evangelism

I have constantly been aware that one of the occupational hazards of a bishop is a preoccupation with administration and tinkering with Church structures, and bricks and mortar. Another is to suppose that we carry the whole weight of responsibility for the Church. But it was our Lord Jesus who said, 'I will build my Church' (Matt. 16:18). We do not do it. What a comfort and encouragement this is. But what a warning! Church building is the prerogative of the Lord. Our calling is to preach the Kingdom of God which He proclaimed. We cannot afford to usurp a role which is His alone.

The purpose of God in renewing His Church with Pentecostal experience and power is that it may speedily accomplish the Great Commission encapsulated for us in Acts 1:8, where the risen Lord gave a promise and a command saying, 'you shall receive power when the Holy Spirit has come upon you; and you shall be my witnesses in Jerusalem and in all Judea and Samaria and to the end of the earth'. What this meant is unfolded for us in the rest of the book of Acts. Is it a wonder that charismatic groups which are not channelling the power of the Spirit for evangelism, edification and discipleship become ingrown, preoccupied with certain gifts for gifts' sake, become stunted, shrivelled up or even arrogant and heretical? The purpose of renewal in the Spirit is power evangelism, including preaching, healing and deliverance – the 'PhD' ministry.

During the last three years the Diocese of Singapore has encouraged and co-ordinated mission teams led by clergy or lay people to other countries for short periods of about two to four weeks. Most of the lay people have been in full-time employment, and have taken their vacation leave, and paid their own airfare to participate in these missions. When this outreach first began we had about forty people moving out to neighbouring countries during the month of June. Since then the number has increased and teams move out at any time during the year.

Adequate preparation has to be made for each trip. Team members are usually given a week's intensive preparation to face cultural, language, and religious barriers. Our teams communicate through mime or interpretation where language is a barrier. They always work in concert with local churches, but they also move out to evangelise in public places and even in red-light districts.

The results have been remarkable and a challenge to further endeavour. The recent teams sent to Thailand saw over two hundred people receive Christ. Some remarkable healing and deliverance also took place. The teams visiting the Philippines last year brought many congregations to new life in the Holy Spirit. One of our parishes continues to help in

Church planting in the Riau Islands in Indonesia. Other teams have been to Malaysia, India, Sri Lanka and even countries beyond Asia.

Many of our people who have experienced power evangelism are considering responding to a call to the full-time ministry. Over a year ago when I first invited those who were thinking about the full-time ministry to come to the episcopal residence for fellowship, about forty people turned up. About half of these are now exercising such a ministry, and some of them are serving overseas. We continue to invite, encourage and guide these precious people at our quarterly fellowship. Some of our parishes have regular meetings for those in the congregation seeking the Lord's mind about responding to a full-time ministry. At one of these meetings I was asked what percentage of the Church's membership should be expected to respond to the full-time ministry. My snap answer was ten per cent, based on the tithing principle. This seemed to strike the people as correct.

Evangelistic outreach continues on the home front in Singapore as only twelve per cent of the population are Christian. A great variety of methods are being used so that we may by all means save some. God willing, Singapore will be preserved as a springboard from which His people move out with His Word in the power of the Spirit.

The Durian Tree

In my garden stands an old durian tree riddled with parasites and with 'pests' like squirrels. The durian is a thorny fruit, either loved or detested by people because of its unique, strong flavour. For some time it had not borne fruit, and I had every reason not to expect fruit. One day we noticed fruit on it. Our office staff got excited about it. We tried to count the fruits on the tree and came up with different estimates. I was certain there would be at least a hundred durians. One of my staff thought that there would be at least four hundred durians. We began to pick durians even before the beginning of the usual durian season, and in four weeks picked 526 durians, each weighing from a half to three kilogrammes!

Then the Word of the Lord came to me: 'You see this durian tree; it is old. It is riddled with all sorts of plant parasites, animal pests, and even human intruders to get at the fruit. You have no reason to expect it to bear fruit, but I have made it fruitful and nothing can stop it. I have given you the season of fruitfulness. It is harvest time. Pick the fruit urgently or else it will rot and be lost. Satisfy yourselves in the abundance of my choicest fruit, and rejoice in the sharing of it. Before the durian stalls have appeared at the roadside you have already enjoyed and shared its fruit. In your abundance you will know how precious is each fruit. I have made your tree a leader in fruitfulness, in time, in quality and in quantity. But you are only one tree among all my many trees. The Anglican Church is an old tree, "by schisms rent asunder, by heresies distressed". Yet it will become fruitful when my life blood flows through it, as my Spirit invigorates and renews it. Be open-ended to what I have still to do with you.'

Notes

1. Michael Harper, *Bishop's Move* (Hodder & Stoughton, 1978).

Appendix Diocesan Lay Training

Module 1. How to pray effectively
Module 2. How to know the will of God
Module 3. How to live victoriously
Module 4. How to handle the Word of God
Module 5. How to exercise the gifts of the Spirit
Module 6. How to manage your resources effectively
Module 7. How to witness in the home

Module 8. How to counsel
Module 9. How to lead a person to Christ
Module 10. How to follow up a new Christian
Module 11. How to lead a person into the Baptism in the Holy Spirit
Module 12. How to pray for the sick
Module 13. How to pray
Module 14. How to lead a Home Cell Group
Module 15. How to lead the Christian life at work
Module 16. How to build a Christian family
Module 17. How to be a leader in the Church
Module 18. How to lead worship
Module 19. How to preach
Module 20. How to meet the needs of our community

A RENEWED COMMUNITY AS A SIGN OF THE KINGDOM

LESSONS FROM ST MICHAEL-LE-BELFREY, YORK, ENGLAND

The Rev Graham Cray

The work of renewal at St Cuthbert's Church, York, began on 1 July 1965, when David and Anne Watson moved from Cambridge to York where David was to take charge of the congregation. In 1966 they began to teach consistently about the person and work of the Holy Spirit in renewal. The story of the growth at St Cuthbert's and the eventual move to the larger church of St Michael-le-Belfrey has been outlined by David himself in *You are my God*. It is not my purpose to retell the story, but rather to outline some of the lessons and principles learned or being learned through twenty-one years of seeking to follow the Spirit as a congregation. Each local congregation should be a community experiencing ongoing renewal. To that extent it is a sign of the Kingdom of God.

Definitions

The Kingdom of God is interpreted in so many different ways in the Church today that I need to begin by defining my terms. Jesus taught us to pray the simplest definition of the Kingdom: '[Your] Kingdom come' means, '[Your] will be done on earth as it is in heaven' (Matt. 6:10). The biblical writers express this not only in individual terms but especially in terms of restored relationships. 'The Kingdom is the new order which began in Christ and which will be completed by Him, wherein all relationships will be put right, and not only that between God and man, but also those between people, nations, sexes, generations and races, and that between man and nature.'[1] Because the Kingdom has begun in Christ, but is not yet completed in Him, a sign of the Kingdom is an experience of relationships restored today in Christ, which points forward to the day when every knee shall bow to Him and every relationship be put right. A sign of the Kingdom is an experience of what is already possible in Christ by the Spirit which is a pointer to the Kingdom in its fullness. In this sense, a renewed community is a sign of the Kingdom, provided that the experience of restored relationships motivates the members to reach out to God's broken world.

Howard Snyder has written, 'Whenever a Christian is working in Jesus' name for reconciliation in the world, working to mend the brokenness of the world and to heal the sickness caused by the fall, and where such activity springs from Christian love and a true sense of Christian vocation, there God is at work and there is a sign of the Kingdom.'[2] The Holy Spirit who both forms and renews the Church[3] is sent by Jesus to make the Kingdom present. 'The Spirit, we might say, is the presentness of the coming Kingdom. Where he is, the Kingdom is, so that to have the Spirit is to have part and lot in the Kingdom here and now. Or to put it another way, the Spirit is the executive ambassador or steward of the Kingdom: his power and authority are those of the Kingdom; his operation is the exercise of kingly rule.'[4] If the Kingdom implies the restoration of all relationships in a broken world, and if it is experienced through the power of the Holy Spirit, then renewal is always for the sake of mission. The Church exists for the Kingdom of God (Matt. 6:33; 16:18–19).

Renewal by the Holy Spirit is not just to restore apparently lifeless or tradition-bound congregations to be part of a vibrant new Christian sub-culture. It is to restore the Church to the work of the Kingdom. Renewal in the Church is for the sake of the world. A paper prepared for a previous Lambeth conference concluded 'Mission without renewal is hypocrisy.'[5] If renewal in the Spirit is for mission, then the gifts of the Spirit, the practical tools the Spirit gives for the task, are as much for ministry in the world as within the Church. 'In exercising spiritual gifts, we are involved in the restoration of God's perfect work in creation. An activity can only be characterised as a spiritual gift when it assists in the restoration of creation and contributes to the restoration of a sick world.'[6] In this way, the gifts and ministries of individual Christians may be understood as signs of the Kingdom, but only if they are rooted in and arise out of, the life of a congregation whose quality of relationships is such that it is in itself a sign of the Kingdom.

A Journey

After twenty-one years, it is comparatively easy to write down the theology and definitions given above. This, however, was not the understanding with which our congregation began. Our vision and theology have developed over the years. Any Church beginning to experience renewal is likely to pay more attention to what is happening than to why it is happening. The newness and freshness of experience of the Holy Spirit is inevitably the immediate focus of attention. God begins by bringing new life and reality to our particular tradition and limited set of expectations. Later, He begins to expand our horizons. The initial characteristics of renewal at St Cuthbert's were an emphasis on personal conversion and personal empowering by the Spirit, a growing sense of family, and the discovery of spiritual gifts as a means of ministering to one another, particularly in meetings. There was an excitement about prayer and Bible study, and from the beginning an understanding of the essential connection between the power of the Spirit and evangelism. All of these are, and will always remain essential. In another sense, however, for some of us the Holy Spirit of God was being invited into a Conservative Evangelical world to help Conservative Evangelical things to be done better by adding some Pentecostal emphases. The Spirit always begins with our world and our expectations, but then begins to draw us into His world and His expectations. Over the years, this has led to various insights which make up the remainder of this chapter. We have never departed from our evangelical roots, but rather like Abraham, we were setting out on a journey without always knowing where we were being led. Any genuine renewal involves a renewal of the mind (Rom. 12:2). If one aspect of the work of the Spirit is to guide us into all truth (John 16:13), we should expect a continually developing understanding of God's purposes.

Relationships

The journey into truth never stops. Nevertheless, after the initial experience of renewal, a new sense of corporate identity begins to emerge within a congregation. In one sense a congregation is developing into a community. From this point on, the effectiveness of all future developments in ministry or mission will depend upon the quality of personal relationships and commitment within the church. The renewal of the Spirit needs to be experienced personally and in that sense individually, but it is essentially a corporate reality. As a friend from the Community of Celebration put it, 'The sign of the Holy Spirit's coming and abiding in a particular place is the emergence of a common life. An openness to one another, a sharing in each other's lives, becomes the pattern rather than the exception.'[7] This sums up our experience and our aspirations. We have experienced enough of this quality of life together to know that it is the fellowship of the Holy Spirit. We have also failed one another sufficiently often to know that we are still immature in the business of sharing our lives.

For twenty-one years the congregation at St Michael's has been reminded of Jesus' command that we are to love one another as He has loved us (John 13:34). This involves a commitment to Christ, but Christ who dwells in my brother or sister by the Holy Spirit. It requires us to be willing continually to take the initiative in establishing relationships knowing that we only love Him because He first loved us (1 John 4:10–11). When relationships are broken it involves the responsibility to put things right, whether we regard ourselves as the innocent or offending party (Matt. 5:23–24, 18:15). It involves an unlimited willingness to forgive (Matt. 18:21–35).

It involves a commitment to remain truthful and honest with one another (Eph. 4:15), to serve one another humbly with our words, possessions, homes and time.[8] Above all it requires us to be open and vulnerable to one another and to share ourselves, not just our beliefs and tasks (1 Thess. 2:8). All of this is centred on the cross. Our unity is possible only because of the cross (Eph. 2:11–22; 4:32). It is maintained only by the Holy Spirit who is the power of the resurrection enabling us to live the lifestyle of the cross with one another (Eph. 1:19–20, 3:10). John Howard Yoder has suggested that the only imitation of Christ the New Testament requires of us is the imitation of His death.[9] Certainly in the New Testament, the example of the cross is applied to the bearing of injustice, mutual forgiveness, not insisting on rights, sharing possessions, refusing special status with leadership, and mutual submission within marriage.[10] We have learned that every aspect of ministry and mission is dependent in part on the quality of our relationships.[11]

The Fruit of Relationships

a) Worship

Worship is both the first calling of a church and a vital ingredient in its life. The quality of corporate worship provides an essential sense of security for the majority of the members.[12] Members of a congregation need to feel at home with both the style of worship and their fellow worshippers. This basic security is the context for expectant faith. Because the congregation is secure in the worship of God, its members can develop a high level of faith and expectancy and an ability to respond positively to the challenges and interventions of God through the ministries of word, sacrament and spiritual gifts. We have learnt that corporate worship depends on the depth of our relationships. Harmony of voice comes out of harmony of lives. As a consequence, our choir and other worship ministry groups spend as much time each week in sharing, prayer and informal worship together as they do in formal rehearsal. All those involved in any aspect of our evening service spend half an hour in prayer and worship together an hour before the start of the service. In that time our aim is to move from being a group of rushed individuals who have hurried to church, into a sense of interdependence, sensitivity to one another and to God, and of the priority of worship. As we pray we expect the Holy Spirit to speak to us about the service which is to follow. Each of us is responsible for seeing that our relationships are right with our fellow worshippers before the service begins.

The whole congregation is formed into a network of geographically based house groups, and every house group or ministry group is expected to develop this quality of relationships. This has introduced an element of gentleness and sensitivity into our worship. We find much charismatic worship insensitive and triumphalist. Part of safety in worship is that each worshipper is able to be real. Those who are struggling with pain and difficulty can worship by offering God their pain silently while others sing praise, rather than having to pretend that everything is going well by switching on a smile and singing up-tempo choruses. This approach to worship has released the creative gifts of many of the congregation. We have professional musicians, actors and designers in the congregation, but many of our songs, sketches, banners and dances have been produced by those with no formal training, helped at times by the professionals, but helped much more by the shared lives and mutual trust in the composition workshop, banner group or the writing resource group. Our Director of Music, Andrew Maries has written, 'The worship of a loving and unified community of Christians is the deepest we can experience outside of heaven – and it is what God intended for us . . . An important part of worship is therefore to live in love with our brothers and sisters.'[13]

b) Leadership

Rapidly increasing numbers, a growing sense of family and study of the New Testament patterns of leadership led in 1970 to the appointment of lay elders. We are convinced that New Testament leadership in the local church is always shared. At present, there are eighteen elders, including the three clergy and two others, employed full time by the Parochial Church Council. Of the eighteen, eleven are men and seven women. Elders are nominated by the congregation, appointed by the Vicar and serve for three years with the possibility of re-appointment. At the start of each three-year period, they are commissioned at a main service by the bishop. We have not only had to share leadership – that was just the beginning – over the years we have had to redefine our whole understanding of leadership. The sequence of events was inevitable and I believe appropriate. (It is unrealistic to attempt to re-write the past on the basis of hindsight.)

We began with a strong leader in David. He gathered round him a group of elders primarily committed to share and support his ministry. That group began to share more equally and fully with him the oversight and decision-making of the congregation. This stage continued, I believe, for longer than it should and the congregation became very dependent upon the eldership, whereas leadership is meant to help each Christian to take responsibility for himself before God in a fellowship of mature interdependent relationships. At this stage, we found we had replaced the one-man ministry as the cork in the bottle with a shared ministry having the same effect. It was when we took seriously the servant nature of Christian leadership that we were able to release the ministries of far more members of the congregation than before.

A primary role of leadership within a congregation is to

discern, encourage, support and order the gifts of each of the members. Leaders are not to 'do' ministry but to equip the saints to do the ministry (Eph 4:11–12). This involves being willing to trust others with ministries that we know we could do better. The clearest example of this was David Watson's willingness to trust the ordained leadership of the congregation to me, giving me the genuine and full authority and supporting me fully in the joys and sorrows of the following years.[14] The other essential role of leadership is to model or be the living example of the vision God has given a congregation. By vision, I do not primarily mean: 'what is the next step?' or 'what are the priorities?' Vision is not the answer to the question, 'What are we to do?' It is the answer to the question, 'What are we?' What are the distinctive features of the work of God in a particular congregation out of which the rest of the ministry will arise? If shared leadership comes out of an understanding of the central place of relationships in the Body of Christ, then the role of those leaders is to be a corporate expression of that quality of relationships. Mutual submission, commitment, openness and vulnerability are central. How leadership decisions are made is as important as what decisions are made. All of this does have to be placed in realistic structures. When our eldership was no more than twelve, one central gathering of all the elders was all that was necessary. Now we are eighteen, and likely to increase again at the next appointment, sub-division of responsibility and fellowship in smaller groups has become essential. Structure can never create life, but the wrong structure, (often the right one years before) can seriously hinder life.[15]

c) Women in leadership

For five years the leadership of St Cuthbert's was primarily in the hands of David and Anne Watson. When the first elders were appointed in 1970, they were exclusively men, according to the traditional interpretation of passages in 1 Corinthians and 1 Timothy.[16] For some years, the ministry of women in the church was restricted, in practice, to: work with children, catering, flower arranging, banners, dance and prophecy. As our understanding of leadership, by men or women, became less one of ruling and more one of serving, less one of caring for people and more one of teaching people to care for one another, so women were drawn into the leadership of our area groups. At first they were in partnership with their husbands, but later single or married women led in their own right. All of this involved a long, slow process of change – partial changes of insight, resulting in changes of practice. The changes in our understanding of ministry led many of us to question whether or not we were interpreting the Pauline passages correctly. By 1977, eldership was the only role from which women were excluded by definition. By that time, (before I was Vicar) I had become convinced that we were wrong. That same year, both Michael Harper and George Carey put the same opinion into print.[17] Meanwhile, David was writing *I Believe in the Church* and had received a number of gracious, but strongly critical responses to his original draft on the ministry of women. As a result of this, he also radically revised his position.[18] By the time of my appointment as Vicar in 1978, both David and I were convinced that the eldership should be as open to women as to men. After teaching in 1980, to which the congregation responded with substantial nominations for a number of women, the first three women became elders. Three years later, the number increased to seven. In 1982, a woman was appointed as the first full-time administrator and the following year the decision was made to appoint a deaconess rather than a second curate, with the proviso that only a woman suitably gifted for public teaching would be appropriate.

I have outlined the history of these developments in some detail to make it clear that a long, slow process was involved, and that our experience of a new quality of relationship led us eventually to revise our understanding of leadership in general, and the place of women in particular. However, it is one thing to change theology; it is another to change inner attitudes. Some months after the first women joined the team, one of them approached me to ask if I realised how difficult they were finding the elders meetings. When I asked what was wrong, she replied, 'Have you men any idea how you relate to one another?' The patterns of an all-male team took time to change, and are still in the process of changing six years later. But the partnership of men and women in the overall leadership of the congregation has immensely enriched the quality and sensitivity of our decision-making and pastoral care. There is no evidence that we have lost men from the congregations in any numbers as a result of these developments. (There was a painful split over a number of issues including the ministry of women, which I will come to later.) However, the vast majority of the congregation was clearly committed to the change and many men found it a great relief to be delivered from a view of male authority which had caused considerable tension.

d) Children

The changes in our understanding of leadership and the ministry of women were long, slow ones. The impact on our understanding of the place of children came far more quickly. Within nine months of David and Anne's arrival, morning worship each Sunday was a Family Service. All-age worship, where we experience being the family of God together and refuse to hive children off, leaving the grown-ups to the 'adult' business of worship, has been our experience for twenty years. This created a sense of family and Sunday morning is still the service at which the core St Michael's members of all ages are most fully represented. This is a family service, not a children's service. Our understanding is that our children are not 'the church of tomorrow' but fellow members of the Body of Christ today on the basis of their baptism. As with every other age group in the church, it is their right to have the worship accessible to them and to participate without unfairly dominating. Children up to the age of twelve choose a song or chorus to be sung on the nearest Sunday to their birthday; they help take the offering, are involved with their parents in leading prayers, play in the orchestra that accompanies the organ, contribute dance, drama or mime, make banners and read the lesson.

It was during an early attempt to teach some children a dance as a contribution to Family Service that Anne Watson realised that something further was needed. She saw that the children did not know how to relate to one another as brothers and sisters in Christ, and that competition was a much stronger drive in them than partnership. As a result, the Children's Workshop was set up. Starting after their first full term at school, and ending when they move to secondary school, our children meet together each Friday night. This is not a traditional Sunday school, and it is aimed entirely at the children of believing parents who are regular worshippers with us.

The difficulty with the traditional Sunday school approach is that it often attempts to reach parents through children, resulting at one stage in large Sunday schools throughout Britain, packed with the children of those who did not attend church and who eventually decided that as their parents did not attend church there was no reason why they should attend Sunday school. This was a logic to which most parents had no answer and the whole process resulted in the inoculation of many children against a genuine encounter with Christ. More recently, the increasingly secular atmosphere of British culture has meant that fewer and fewer non-church-attending parents would send their children in the first place. The real casualties in this system were the children of Christian homes who had been raised to trust in Christ from their earliest memories, but who were lost in the crowd of children who had no such background or faith and were in effect treated as little unbelievers along with the rest. We believe that one of our greatest responsibilities as a church is to nurture the children of Christian homes, not only in their relationship with Jesus, but in their relationships with one another, and their adult brothers and sisters in the church. Children's Workshop does not centre on formal teaching, but involves cooperation in music, dance, drama and non-competitive games in the context of worship and all-age sharing groups. There, the children share what Jesus has said to them or done for them and the things that have mattered most to them in the preceding week. In this context they are taught to pray for one another. As these children grow older and move on to our Pathfinder group and youth fellowship, they are at an age at which it is more appropriate to invite their non-Christian friends, who are then introduced into an essentially Christian setting rather than a gathering of non-Christians with Christian leaders trying to evangelise them. The two foundations for this understanding of not only ministry to children but the ministry of children, are the Pauline passages about the Body of Christ and the inter-dependence of its members, and the teaching of Jesus about the value and significance of children in the Kingdom of God (Matt. 18:1–14, 19:13–15). Many of us found it very painful to break away from long established patterns of independence and defensiveness. We want our children to learn a better way from the beginning.

e) Counselling

Committed, trusting relationships give people a sense of safety and security. In that context they are able to begin to face hurts and fears which until that time had been consciously or unconsciously suppressed. Equally the vulnerability of close relationships means that we are easily wounded by one another and find only too often that our response is not a Christ-like one of love and forgiveness. In both of these ways, renewed relationships result in a need for personal healing. In addition, the experience of personal empowering by the Spirit often results in a sense of being sifted; of aspects of the darker side of our personality being brought to the light for repentance or healing. Each of these demands that the Body of Christ must not only be a safe place but also a skilled and gifted place for healing. Many of our congregation have experienced a simple but deep inner healing. Either in their own prayer, or in the presence of a pastor, they have asked the Holy Spirit to bring to mind the traumatic memories from the past which still cripple or restrict their freedom in Christ in the present. The memory may return as a reminder of an event or sometimes as a reliving of the original emotions.

It is often sufficient simply to bring the whole situation to the foot of the cross in prayer, to repent of sin, to forgive whoever has sinned against us, and to ask for healing. Much past pain can be taken privately to God without the help of another. However, we would encourage anyone who has done this to share what they have done with a brother or sister in whom they trust. We all need someone to encourage, support and challenge us in the much harder task of establishing a new pattern of greater wholeness in the area of life which has been affected. My own understanding is that such inner blocks may be due to a number of causes: to personal sin needing repentance, to the sins of others who have wounded us, to emotional deprivation and a lack of love and affirmation (rather than to specific wounding incidents), to trauma experienced by our mother when we were in the womb, or to trauma such as untimely death in previous generations, or more often to family patterns passed down the generations. On occasions, there is demonic origin, usually related to personal or family involvement in the occult. (In this case we restrict ministry to the elders on my direct authority, after consultation with the bishop in apparently severe cases.)

Some years ago, we reached the point when our general ministry of inner healing and pastoral care was not proving sufficient. Some members of the congregation had long-term problems for which we had not been able to provide significant help. It was at that time that Sharon Stinson, one of our full-time pastoral workers, began to develop counselling skills and gifts which integrated inner healing and the ministry of spiritual gifts with insights from psychology and psychotherapy interpreted from a Christian viewpoint. Clinical theology, transactional analysis and Gestalt therapy have all contributed to this, as have courses in Christian listening, biblical meditation and contemplative prayer. Having sought out these insights in her own counselling ministry, Sharon is now able to train others in them. A small proportion of our members have found this development difficult to accept, asking if the Lord and His Spirit were not enough and why did we need insights from 'the world', but most have recognised the biblical foundation, the context of prayer and deep relationships and the resulting changes in people's lives. We do not have answers for everyone. There have been some we have been unable to help and others whom we have referred for more specific professional help, but the overall health of the congregation has vastly improved as a result of this ministry.

Our understanding of worship, leadership, the ministry of women, the place of children and the counselling and healing ministry in the Body of Christ have all come as a direct consequence of our experience of renewed community. They are a sign of the Kingdom in that the worship points to our first loyalty, namely to the King, and the other aspects give visible demonstration of the new relationships of the Kingdom.

The Fruit of Failure!

The Kingdom of God is a gift, not an achievement (Luke 12:32). It is entered through many hardships (Acts 14:22). Our experience is that 'joy and pain are woven fine'. There is pain on the road to 'success'. Our struggles to release women into an equal and just place in ministry are an example of this. However, there is also the pain of failure, the experience of the negative and destructive, out of which paradoxically God has taught us the deepest lessons and brought the most mature fruit. Failure, like vulnerability, is not faced easily by Western Christians. 'We never see God in failure, but only in success, a strange attitude for people who have the cross at the centre of their faith.'[19] Three major traumas stand out in our history: the closure of the Mustard Seed Shop, the split which resulted in the setting up of a house church, and David Watson's illness and death.

a) The Mustard Seed

The Mustard Seed Shop which opened in 1976, closed in a painful failure of relationships and mutual trust three years later. The shop had been intended as a sign of the Kingdom, a place where both York people and tourists could encounter the atmosphere of Christ's Kingdom while having a meal, or while browsing through the various gift or craft goods. An immense amount of good was achieved. The pain of the ending must not be allowed to obscure the quality of what was done in those years. It is not my intention to retell the story, but there was eventually a multiple failure of relationships both between those directly involved and equally between the leaders of the project and the elders. We learned painfully that the leaders and majority of members of a church need to be wholeheartedly behind any major ministry initiative from the beginning if those in the front line are to have any sort of security. It is no good supporting a ministry when it is going well, and then criticising it and saying you had doubts about it in the first place when it is in crisis.

We also learned the necessity of supplying proper pastoral support to work that seemed established and appeared to have less need of it than at the beginning, and that the greater the responsibility leaders have, the more necessary it is they be genuinely answerable to others. Despite the pain and hurt, the vision for a Christian centre or coffee shop has never died and we are now involved in negotiations with the Diocese about such a use for a newly redundant parish church. We have learned that the vision for a project and the call to it can genuinely be from God and yet we can still lack the wisdom to put that vision into effect. God in His grace has restored this vision to us but to see it live again we will need to learn the lessons of our previous failure.

b) A painful split

The most painful trauma which our church had experienced to date came in November 1980, when some members including one elder and a number of experienced house-group leaders left us, eventually to form a 'house church'. It was an experience of intense pain, a tearing. At that time, the church had had fifteen years of teaching on committed relationships. To have some who had been close friends for years leave in such a traumatic way was almost unbearable. The majority who remained felt betrayed and deserted. Those who left felt they had been pushed out and that there was no further place for them. The pain was equally great on both sides, but each side felt its own pain too greatly to be objective.

A number of issues triggered the split. The first was the question of what God was saying to St Michael's. Those who left felt that He was calling us beyond our emphasis on relationships to face the challenge of intercessory prayer and spiritual warfare. I and many who remained believed that relationships were the context in which we heard the various things that the Spirit of God was saying, which included the emphases of the others, but was not limited to them. Central to the issue was the understanding of leadership. Our new emphasis on authority as servanthood ran counter to the growing concern of the others for a restoration of pastoral authority in the church through some form of personal shepherding. The final straw was the admission of women to the eldership.

At that time, perhaps twenty-five people left, which was a small proportion of the whole church, but because of our emphasis on mutual commitment, that made it no less painful. By the grace of God, our relationships are now reconciled. It took fully five years for the pain to settle, but we are now able to pray for one another as churches, to ask God's blessing on one another and for the ministers to share in a monthly fraternal. What we did not have the maturity to see at the time was that a minority spirituality had emerged within St Michael's that could not properly co-exist with that of the majority. The group who left had little sense of calling to the Church of England, whereas St Michael's is called to be part of the renewal of the Church of England from within the Church of England. Had we all had the wisdom and foresight, our brothers and sisters could have been released with our blessing to fulfil their own vision without the mutual sense of tearing and betrayal. Obviously an Anglican parish cannot plant a house church in another parish, but we could have separated graciously rather than have contested over the future of St Michael's.

c) David's leaving and death

David Watson's illness and death was a different experience of 'failure'. The Mustard Seed and the split were evidence that our ability to love fell far short of our vision of loving. David's death was a different sort of reminder that the Kingdom is not yet, as well as already. In *You are my God* David describes his leaving York in 1982 as a form of bereavement. This deep sense of loss was equally felt by many in the congregation. However, the move was seen as much for our sake as for the sake of David's future ministry. Dave wrote, 'We felt that the time had come for us as "parents" to make room for others to take over, without us looking over their shoulders all the time to see how they were getting on. Apart from any other reason, it was primarily for the future health and growth of the congregation of St Michael's that we knew we ought to move.' Thus in God's sovereignty, the founding figure of the work at St Michael's left York before terminal illness and death took him from us permanently.

The sense of bereavement after seventeen years began with the leaving and continued with the illness. Despite thirteen months of prayer, including at one stage, six consecutive weeks of special meetings for the whole church, the elders who were fully informed of David's progress, never once felt that they had heard God say that he would be healed. The pain was very great. The healing ministry, however actively pursued, rests ultimately in the sovereignty of God, and though there were many specific answers to prayer, the one we most longed for was not to be. So our church has had to face the reality of suffering and death alongside the realities of healing and new life. If Christian experience does not include some element of suffering and despair, we become the sign of the Kingdom that is irrelevant and out of reach, rather than one that has broken into the pain of the present but also points to the certainty of God's future.

d) Too far too fast?

Another area of pain and difficulty was directly related to a strength. Many congregations are conservative, deeply resistant to change. An investigation into St Michael's carried out by the Archbishop's Council on Evangelism, showed a very high level of openness to change. We had indeed been learning to follow the Spirit, and it is very easy to reflect with the benefit of hindsight, but almost certainly we went too far too fast, regarding some areas of lifestyle.

One of these areas of change was the creation of extended households. The first extended household was formed in the Rectory by David and Anne Watson in 1973. Others were formed in 1975 and at one stage about ten were in existence. This was a very creative time in which many individuals were supported and released for ministry and in which many of us experienced God in the fellowship of the Holy Spirit at an entirely new level. As one of the last couples to be drawn in, Jackie and I have few regrets about the opening of our home and family relationships to others. We have needed periods as just a nuclear family, making space to love ourselves as a family if we were to love those who at other times were to live with us. But once having shared that part of life with Christian brothers and sisters we would never want permanently to lock it up again. Many core members of our congregation had their spiritual life and vision formed in those years. There was also pain, difficulty and some mistakes. The pain was inevitable. The closer you draw to one another, the less you are able to hide your true self, especially those parts of it which you find hard to acknowledge. Some positive pastoral trauma is an inevitable result of this way of living. Some mistakes were made in that some families entered too quickly and lightly into a style of life whose implications they had not fully considered. Shared ownership of houses and joint financial arrangements should be the last stage in the development of an extended household. Financial commitment needs to express the actual level of personal commitment and mutuality. It cannot be a commitment imposed to create commitment.

After some years, the households began to disband. This was never a conscious policy decision. Some had not been well founded and inevitably ran out of steam. Others heard the call of God to come into being and after a number of years, were equally sure they heard His call to stop. Others disbanded as young couples who had begun together before they had children began to have their families, and even large shared houses did not provide sufficient space. Just as the Spirit called this style of life into being, so I believe He knew when it would become counter-productive to the work of the Kingdom among us. After some years, it was clear that some in the congregation were threatened by this style of life and were focusing on the element of pain experienced by those who shared their lives deeply. They were writing off the households as only causing the church problems. This was not totally without foundation, but it failed to recognise that anyone who lives his life intimately with other Christians must be vulnerable and will experience pain as well as growth. Perhaps more significantly, other members of the congregation were pointing to the households as though to say, 'We have community in our church – they do it.' The households were almost living as a community vicariously on behalf of the rest of the congregation.

In the end, I believe the grain of wheat which was the households had to fall into the ground and die so that the whole Body of Christ could have a far deeper sense of the shared life which is Christian fellowship. The fruit and gain of that time is still with us. Household as one practical way of expressing fellowship and releasing ministry is still a viable option among us, but in the context of a bigger version of shared life. Many still find this threatening, but overall I am convinced that the household period contributed far more gain than loss to the long-term health and vitality of the congregation.

In 1978, David gave a series of sermons entitled 'Living in

an age of hunger' as a preparation for the publication of the British edition of Ronald Sider's book *Rich Christians in an Age of Hunger* for which he wrote the foreword. The emphasis on simple lifestyle which came out of this series was not easily received by the congregation. The biblical teaching was sufficiently clear but the challenge to lifestyle was painful and many could not see how personally living more simply would make any difference to those in the Third World. Looking back, I believe that the congregation was receiving one challenge more than it could take. Our present emphasis on the Kingdom and social responsibility would probably never have been possible without it, but at the time, the series did not have the impact that David would have hoped. Overall, the congregation was tired after years of rapid growth and rapid change. At that time we had pioneered so many areas of congregational renewal and evangelistic ministry that we found it very difficult to find peers who could relate to us as equals and minister to us. Everyone we encountered expected us to minister to them. The pain of the closure of the Mustard Seed and the split were in this context.

e) Receiving as well as giving

A further sign of the Kingdom is that the King does not leave His people in need without coming to their aid. The Kingdom is expressed in His sovereignty and His action. His people express the fruit of His actions. In 1981, John Wimber, whom David had met while teaching at Fuller Theological Seminary, brought a team of his people to minister to us for five days. During this time many individuals received a fresh anointing of the Spirit and inner healing and in some cases, dramatic physical healing. However, the major impact was a healing of the church. We asked our visitors to minister first to the leaders of the church and then open it up to the rest of the congregation. As eldership families, we asked John and his team to minister to us publicly in the presence of the congregation and the consequence was a healing of the pain and tiredness and a restoration of energy and strength to continue to follow the Spirit. If we had not been able to receive at that stage, I do not believe that the congregation would have coped as it did with David's leaving and death.

The great contemporary writers on community like Dietrich Bonhoeffer and Jean Vanier[20] point out the stages in the development of Christian community. Inevitably it begins with an ideal, drawn from Scripture but without true knowledge of one's own ability to live a quality of relationships which are only possible by the grace of the Spirit. There must follow a period of disillusion, an experience of failure and of coming to an end of one's own resources. Out of that pain and failure and death comes a new strength, a new vision and a new quality of community. This is not a once-for-all experience, but a cycle which in small ways and large ways has been repeated for us in the last twenty-one years. Its clearest fruit to date is that as a congregation we are no longer monochrome as we used to be. St Michael's is no longer a place full of 'people like us'. There is a greater balance of background, education and spirituality.

We are aware that we are called to live in the tension between old ways and new insights, between the various biblical demands on our time and between the different needs and ministries within a large church. We are beginning to understand the need to live in the tension between some of the opposed viewpoints of a divided universal Church, and to hold together within our own community emphases which are not normally seen together in one congregation. The balance between intercessory and contemplative prayer, between liturgy and spontaneity, between word and sacrament, between evangelism and social responsibility, between unity and different callings, between the ministry of spiritual gifts and counselling which draws on the insights of contemporary psychology, between an emphasis on the healing and power of Christ now, and suffering and patient endurance in the light of the coming Kingdom – these and many other tensions can make life uncomfortable. But could there be a better preparation for mission than to be a people learning within our own numbers, that our unity in Christ is greater than our different emphases on important but secondary matters? Renewal is only authentic if it leads to the healing of a broken Church and mission to a broken world. It is in this light that we need to evaluate any claimed activity of the Spirit.

Relationships Are Not Enough

a) Mission

If renewal is for mission and if a sign of the Kingdom is not only a pointer to the coming Kingdom but an encounter with the present Kingdom, then renewed relationships in themselves are not sufficient. In recent years, we have focused our teaching on the Kingdom of God as defined in the opening paragraphs of this chapter, as a way of exploring the breadth of mission. We understand mission as a threefold cord involving explicit evangelism; the ministry of spiritual gifts, healing, signs and wonders, demonstrating God's grace to non-Christians; and social concern. Some years ago, I asked from the pulpit whether we served our city or just lived off it as an appropriate place in which to put our evangelistic fishing rods and nets. This was, I think, a turning point which broadened our whole understanding of mission. At the time of writing each member of the congregation and each group within it has been asked to identify specific mission priorities and objectives drawn from the teaching about the Kingdom of God. At this point our understanding of leadership, as servant authority to help our members hear God for themselves and support them in responding to Him, has dovetailed with our sense of call to mission. Leaders are working to help the Church hear and fulfil a call to ministry, but ministry which is now understood as much in the world as in the Church. We have always had an emphasis on evangelism, but David Watson's leaving has required us to give less emphasis to public proclamation and more to personal witness with a renewed emphasis on evangelistic growth.

b) Social responsibility

In response to God's call to serve our community, we are becoming involved with the homeless and with young people at risk in our city centre. We are slowly beginning to learn to recognise members' different callings in the world of work, what the Roman Catholics would call the lay apostolate, and to ask our Area Groups to become centres of support for Christian presence and service.

St Michael's has always been a community in which single parents and the divorced find healing and a place to belong. This and our increasing counselling skills should help us provide a city centre counselling and help service based on the Christian centre for which we are preparing at the moment.

c) The arts

York has a strong tradition of the performing arts. The York Festival is the leading arts festival in England and is centred on the York Cycle of Mystery Plays. A major fruit of renewal in St Michael's has been the development of creative and artistic gifts for both worship and mission. The congregation now contains a professional Christian theatre company, a professional mime artist, a number of classical musicians, a producer/arranger with a Christian record company, a mime/music duo involved in evangelism, and many gifted 'amateurs'. We have made five recordings, largely of our own worship material, and performed two full-length musical plays – a stage setting of the Gospel of John, and a number of presentations in music, dance and drama based on different seasons of the church's year. From the congregation have come four books of sketches and advice for church drama groups, two other books on Christianity and the theatre, one on dance and mime, one on music in worship, plus contributions to two books on banners. The integration of music, dance, drama, banners and mime into our worship has become a distinguishing feature taken throughout the world by

David Watson and his team, and resulting in similar groups in scores of other churches.

d) Spiritual gifts

The gift of prophecy has been important in moving us forward. Music and dance were two of the ways in which we celebrated our life together and worshipped together before they became a feature of our evangelism. It was in prophecy that God told us to take what we had onto the streets. We began with music and dance on our church forecourt before services and this has led on to the teams, musicals and other events. York is a tourist city and our ministry in the arts in the setting of an historic church building under the bell tower of York Minster, has given us major evangelistic opportunities. The use of St Michael's for classical concerts and our senior churchwarden's skills as one of the country's leading experts on stained glass have helped us to hold the old and the new together. It was again through prophecy that we heard God's clear call to give a new emphasis to mission, which had a social as well as an evangelistic dimension. We have experienced prophecy which was trivial and unedifying, also that which comforts or challenges the congregation or speaks specifically to the need of an individual, but at certain key times God has spoken to us by His Spirit and His Word in ways which have changed our priorities and set the agenda for several years.

Gradually we are learning that gifts of the Spirit are not just for the Church, but are demonstrations of the lordship of Christ in the world, and are learning to recognise that their context is daily life. Like many involved at the beginning of the charismatic movement, we were so taken by the biblical passages which describe the ministry of gifts among Christians when they meet together, that we failed to give sufficient emphasis to the Gospels and Acts which describe the ministry of spiritual gifts in mission. In particular, we are being challenged to take the healing ministry out from the church into our neighbourhoods and personal relationships.

e) Ecumenical relationships

We are learning that we are not the Body of Christ in York, but simply one comparatively large manifestation of it. The clergy of St Michael's now meet each month with the ministers of seven other churches from four different traditions to pray, share and sometimes plan joint projects. We are also involved in our local Council of Churches and in a growing communication and sharing with the other churches in the city centre, ranging from a house church to Roman Catholics. Partnership with our fellow Christians in York and the complementing of one another's ministries have become increasingly important.

Conclusion

The inadequacies of our church are so painfully obvious to me that I hesitate to use so many words to describe us. But theory which has not been lived is of little value to the Church of God, and any sign of the Kingdom will give evidence of the 'not yet' as much as of the 'already'. When the Spirit renews the Church, he creates community. That community is a sign of the Kingdom if it is both an example of the healed, reconciled and enlarged relationships of the Kingdom, and also a community reaching into its neighbourhood with the claims, power and serving spirit of Jesus Christ its King. Like our salvation, such renewal is not cheap. Having had to review what we have learned of the Spirit, I can see more clearly than ever that we have learned most through the cross.

Notes

1. J. Verkuyl, *The Mission of God and the Missions of the Churches*, (1977) quoted in Orlando E. Costas, *The Integrity of Mission* (Harper & Row, 1979).

2. H. Snyder, *The Community of the King* p. 71 (IVP USA, 1977).
3. 1 Corinthians 12:13.
4. J. Dunn, *Expository Times*, Vol. 82, 1970–71, p. 36–40.
5. Quoted by David Watson.
6. A Bitlinger, *Gifts and Graces* p. 25 (Hodder & Stoughton 1967).
7. Gordon Abbot at a renewal day in Leeds.
8. John 13:14–15; Ephesians 4:29; Hebrews 3:13 and 10:24ff; 1 John 3:16–18; 1 Peter 4:9.
9. J. H. Yoder, *The Politics of Jesus* Chap. 7 (Eerdmans Publishing Co. USA, 1972).
10. 1 Peter 2:22–24; Ephesians 4:32–5:1; 2 Corinthians 8:9; Mark 10:42–45.
11. See also on relationships, David Watson, *Discipleship* Chaps. 2 and 3 (Hodder & Stoughton 1983).
12. Every congregation will contain members whose sense of belonging is 'despite' rather than 'because of' the style of worship, particularly where a geographical parochial system exists.
13. A Maries, *One Heart, One Voice* p. 57 (Hodder & Stoughton 1985) and *Using the Bible in Music* (Bible Society 1983) and David Watson, *I Believe in the Church* Chap. 12 (Hodder & Stoughton 1978).
14. See *David Watson, a Portrait by His Friends* Chap. 9 (Highland Books 1985).
15. For further study: David Watson, *I Believe in the Church* (Hodder & Stoughton 1978); R. Metcalfe, *Sharing Christian Ministry* (Mowbray 1971); J. Bax, *The Good Wine* (Church House Publishing 1986).
16. See Anne Watson's contribution in Shelagh Brown (Ed.), *Married to the Church* (Triangle 1983)
17. Michael Harper, *Let My People Grow* Chap. 8 (Hodder & Stoughton 1977) and George Carey, *I Believe in Man* Chap. 7 (Hodder & Stoughton 1977).
18. Cheryl Forbes, *The Religion of Power* p. 20 (MARC Europe 1986.)
19. See David Watson, *You Are My God* Chap. 14 (Hodder & Stoughton 1986).
20. D. Bonhoeffer, *Life Together* (SCM Press 1954) and Jean Vanier, *Community and Growth* (DLT 1979).